Famous Biographies for Young People

FAMOUS UNDERWATER
ADVENTURERS

FAMOUS UNDERWATER ADVENTURERS

by Frederick Wagner

ILLUSTRATED WITH PHOTOGRAPHS

Dodd, Mead & Company · New York

1963

Grateful acknowledgment is made for permission to use brief quotations from the following sources: *Half Mile Down* by William Beebe, Copyright, 1934, 1951, by William Beebe, reprinted by permission of Duell, Sloan and Pearce; *Beneath Tropic Seas* by William Beebe, Copyright, 1928 by William Beebe, reprinted by permission of G. P. Putnam's Sons; *Earth, Sky and Sea* by Auguste Piccard, translated by Christina Stead, © 1956 by Auguste Piccard, reprinted by permission of Oxford University Press, Inc.; *Seven Miles Down* by Jacques Piccard and Robert S. Dietz, © 1961 by Jacques Piccard and Robert S. Dietz, reprinted by permission of G. P. Putnam's Sons.

Printed in the United States of America
by Vail-Ballou Press, Inc., Binghamton, N.Y.

FOR RALPH,
skin diving
on the
Costa Brava

ACKNOWLEDGMENTS

I WANT to thank Jacques Piccard, Rear Admiral Edward Ellsberg, USNR (Ret.), Vice Admiral C. B. Momsen, USN (Ret.), Dr. Maurice Ewing and Captain Edward L. Beach, USN, for reading, in manuscript, the chapters about themselves. James Dugan kindly looked through the chapter on Captain Cousteau, and Hannes Keller graciously supplied answers to many questions. Their courtesy in helping me avoid factual errors is gratefully acknowledged.

I appreciate the generous cooperation of the following: W. J. Eads, Assistant to the Director, News Office, Columbia University; C. M. Johnson, Head, Technical Information Division, U.S. Navy Electronics Laboratory, San Diego; R. S. Greenbaum, Acting Technical Information Officer, Office of Naval Research, Department of the Navy, Washington; Gene Witmer, Public Information Officer, U.S. Navy Submarine Base, New London; T. M. Little, Lt. (jg), USNR, Public Information Office, Headquarters of the Third Naval District, New York City; Lt. (jg) A. E. Holt, USNR, Still Picture Officer, CHINFO, Department of the Navy, Washington; Mrs. Emery E. Bassett, Librarian, The Submarine Library, Groton; John Tee-Van, General Director, New York Zoological Society; and Daniel J. Scherer, Manager of Publicity, IBM World Trade Corporation.

John L. Lochhead, Librarian, The Mariners Museum, Newport News, and Harold Danziger of Columbia Pictures Corporation were among those who cheerfully helped in the search for photographs. From Trinidad Dr. William Beebe sent permission to use the photograph that originally appeared in *Half Mile Down*.

In tracking down additional material for this book I was

continually amazed by the vast resources of the New York Public Library and by the limitless patience and helpfulness of the staff of the Central Building—in particular those in the Main Reading Room, the Science and Technology Division, and the Microfilm Newspaper Service. All sources consulted are listed in the Bibliography.

My editor, Joe Ann Daly, and my wife, Barbara, were unfailing in their help and encouragement.

FREDERICK WAGNER

New York City

CONTENTS

Illustrations follow page 64

FAMOUS UNDERWATER
ADVENTURERS

EDMOND HALLEY

[1656–1742]

"Nor do I believe any further thing can be hoped or desired in the art of going under Water."
— Edmond Halley on September 23, 1691,
concluding a speech on his underwater
inventions before London's Royal Society

Astronomer, physicist, engineer, statesman, traveler, mariner and underwater adventurer—Edmond Halley left the mark of his genius on every one of the many fields that aroused his interest. This curious, bustling, inventive man is probably best remembered as the discoverer of the path of Halley's Comet, last seen in 1910 and due again in 1986. But this was just one of several dozen feats achieved by this remarkable human being who went through eighty-five years of life exploding ideas like firecrackers.

Even though Halley's underwater inventions, despite his boast, actually left much to be desired, for the point in history at which he stood they were astounding.

As far back as Homer there are records of underwater adventurers—divers seeking pearls or sponges or sunken treasure from shipwrecks. The Persian king and conqueror

Xerxes is said to have used salvage divers. Legend has it that Alexander the Great remained down in a diving bell for three days to watch a giant sea monster pass by. Leonardo da Vinci's notebooks reveal a number of sketches for underwater equipment. Although several diving bells had been built by the middle of the seventeenth century, all of them were clumsy, impractical devices. It took the fertile mind of Edmond Halley to conceive both a diving bell and a diving suit that far surpassed any earlier inventions and pointed the way to future progress.

"This miracle of energy," as one of his friends called him, was born in London on October 26, 1656. He was the son of a prosperous soap-boiler who suffered heavy losses in London's Great Fire of 1666 and suffered even more at the hands of his extravagant, ill-tempered second wife.

At Oxford young Edmond Halley sped brilliantly through a course of studies that included Latin, Greek, Hebrew, Geometry, Navigation and Astronomy, and at the age of nineteen wrote a paper on the orbits of planets that made the scientific world outside Oxford sit up and take notice.

Then he discovered that, although several famous astronomers were charting the stars in the Northern Hemisphere, no one was charting those in the Southern Hemisphere. Interrupting his studies, he sailed off to St. Helena in the South Atlantic, and in two years determined the position of 341 stars. On the voyage home, he noticed the standard quadrant the sailors were using. It was, he decided, imperfect; so he promptly invented a better one. This was typical of his entire life. If Halley saw something that needed doing, he never waited for someone else to do it. No wonder that he was asked, at only twenty-two, to join the most eminent scientists in England as a Fellow of the Royal Society.

In the next decade "this industrious bee" buzzed about on a multitude of projects, personal as well as scientific. Eager to learn more about the work of the famous astronomer Hevelius, Halley went off to Danzig to meet him in person because the mails were too slow in carrying questions. He made a long, thorough and energetic tour of France and Italy. He met, courted and married Mary Tooke (with whom he lived happily until her death fifty-five years later). He took his stepmother to court when she refused to turn over his inheritance after his father's death. He wrote dozens of articles on his scientific observations and discoveries, including his theory of the magnetic compass. And, most important of all, he formed a fast friendship with Isaac Newton.

Newton was as shy and retiring as Halley was boisterous and convivial. Yet Halley, for all his ceaseless hustle, had an encompassing warmth that few could resist. One day Newton mentioned something of his theory about the law of gravitation, but added that he feared to make it public because of controversy and criticism it might arouse. Halley immediately set aside everything he was doing (as usual, he was doing a great deal) and spent the next few years encouraging Newton to publish the now-classic *Principia*. It was Halley who paid all the expenses out of his own pocket (which was none too full). It was Halley who corrected the proofs. And it was Halley who alternately bullied, cajoled and spurred on Newton until the revolutionary work was completed.

Only then did Halley turn back to his own work, ranging from exercises in pure mathematics through verifying the date Julius Caesar landed in Britain to advising his fellow scientists to water their gardens with diluted soapsuds, which, he said, helped plants bear the hard winter better.

Then, in the late 1680's, undistracted by the revolution

that had just brought William III to the throne, he set out to improve current methods of salvage. West Indian divers under the command of the adventurous Captain William Phips had recently recovered a fortune in gold from a wrecked Spanish galleon in the Bahamas. Halley's imagination was stirred— not by the value of the treasure, but by what he considered the unbearable inefficiency of the operation. At best, he said, divers could remain underwater only a very short time, and if they went too deep, the pressure caused blood to gush from their ears and noses.

Crude diving bells had been in use for centuries. The early Greeks had lowered vases with the mouth downward to trap the air within; this whiff of air enabled the sponge divers to stay underwater a few moments longer. Although diving bells by Halley's time were slightly larger than the Greek vases, their capacity remained small and they were anchored in one spot. The diver, to do his work, still had to move about outside the bell holding his breath.

Halley's goal was to let the diver walk about underwater with the same freedom he had on dry land. On March 6, 1689, before the Royal Society, he announced that he planned to build a vastly improved diving bell—a cylinder of copper or wood, four feet high, eight feet in diameter, open at the bottom. Set atop a four-wheeled frame, the bell could be moved from spot to spot underwater by the diver working inside.

The problem, of course, was to keep the bell full of air. Because air is compressible, as the bell went deeper the force of the water would compress the air into a smaller and smaller space. More water then could enter the bell, making it heavier and harder to move. To solve this problem, Halley planned to sink containers of compressed air and open them under the bell, thus forcing the water out. As he did not know whether breathing compressed air would harm the diver, he decided to go underwater to find out.

His opportunity came during the summer of 1691, when he undertook the salvage of what he called the "Guiney frigat" on the Sussex coast. The bell he built was five feet high, of wood coated with lead, carefully balanced with heavy weights so that it would sink evenly. The top, which contained a window of thick, strong, clear glass, was three feet across; the open bottom had a diameter of five feet. Suspended two-and-a-half feet (later only one foot) below the bell was a platform on which he and the other divers stood. Within the bell was a bench to be used when the men got tired or cold. The bell itself, hung from a boom extending from the ship, was lowered into the sea by an arrangement of chains and pulleys.

From May until the middle of August Halley conducted his experimental salvage operations. On each dive he carried along an iron pen and lead plate for taking notes. Every fifteen feet the descent of the bell was halted while the crew aboard ship sent down lead-coated iron-bound casks, each holding about forty gallons of compressed air. The divers hauled these under the bell, let out the air, and sent them back up to the ship.

This procedure forced the water out of the bell and also provided a supply of fresh air. A valve in the top of the bell allowed the hot, stale air to escape. "The Air," said Halley, "would rush with so much violence, as to make the Surface of the Sea boyle, and to cover it with White Foam, notwithstanding the great weight of water over us."

On the first dives, the pressure upon his ears was very painful, "as if a Quill were forcibly thrust into the Hole of the Ear."

But, resourceful as ever, Halley shortly discovered that oil of sweet almonds eased the pain. Almost as unpleasant as the pressure was the white fog that filled the bell as it was being raised. It was as thick as the fog of any London winter and, he said, "likewise would stink like our foggs here." Fortunately it disappeared as the bell broke the surface.

On calm, sunny days these underwater pioneers found they had plenty of light: through the glass in the top came a cherry glow, and the water beneath cast a green reflection over everything inside the bell. One day a diver cut his finger and became terrified when blood gushed forth as a result of the pressure. What fascinated Halley was that the blood looked green, without a trace of red, a phenomenon that was to intrigue many future underwater explorers.

Before the summer was over he reported an adventure that thrilled all England. With two companions, he descended to a depth of sixty feet and remained there for an hour and three-quarters, an almost incredible record for the year 1691. For centuries man had dreamed of exploring the underwater world. Edmond Halley proved that this dream could become a reality.

This record, however, was not Halley's only underwater triumph. In actual practice his original notion of a bell on wheels did not work, so he devised a way to allow the diver to work freely outside the bell—a diving suit which was not significantly improved upon for the next 150 years.

As adventurous in action as he was in thought, Halley insisted on testing the suit himself. For protection against the cold, he first donned triple-thick knit woolen trousers and a jacket. On top of these he put on a leather suit, which had been fitted to his body and made watertight by being dipped in a scalding hot mixture of beeswax, tallow, turpentine and oil.

His helmet, which he called a "Cap of Maintenance," worked

on the same principle as his diving bell. Made of lead, it was heavy enough to sink when empty. To provide stability against the current, Halley added two twelve-pound clogs of lead to his feet and put on a quilted girdle containing heavy lead shot.

A forty-foot pipe led from the cap back to the bell; pressure inside the bell forced air through the pipe whenever the level of the cap was above the level of the water in the bell. A second pipe allowed air to escape from the cap to a container floating above the bell. These pipes were made of hollow wire, with an opening one-sixth inch in diameter. Around each wire Halley sewed thin glove-leather, dipped this in hot oil and beeswax, then folded sheep's guts around it and painted it, and finally added another coat of leather.

In the cap, Halley said, "I at first fixt a plain Glass before the Sight, but soon found that the Vapour of the Breath would make such a Dew on the Surface of the Glass, that it hindered its transparency: To remedy which, I found it necessary to prolong that Side of the Cap that was before the Eyes, and thereby enlarged the Prospect of what was under us."

The greatest disadvantage to this rig was that the diver had to be extremely careful not to tip his "Cap of Maintenance" and flood it. Yet, crude as it was, it worked so well that the only major improvement made over the next century and a half was to connect the air hoses to the surface and pump air down. Then, in 1837, Augustus Siebe, a German-born engineer who had opened a small business in London, invented the "closed dress"—the prototype of our modern diving dress. This consisted of a flexible suit covering everything except the diver's head, hands and feet. The cuffs were watertight, and a rubber collar was fitted to the breastplate. The helmet— equipped with improved inlet and exhaust valves—could be screwed tight to the breastplate with one-eighth of a turn.

Edmond Halley, while working on the "Guiney frigat" down on the Sussex coast, also invented an underwater lantern to provide the diver with illumination. In addition, he devised a mortar that would fire underwater to blow up the decks of a wreck so that divers could carry on salvage more effectively.

Long after the summer of 1691 Halley continued to improve his diving bell and suit and to work on new underwater inventions. In 1693 he reported that he had made a gauge on the principle of a barometer by which divers could judge the depth to which they were descending. In 1716 and again in 1721 he summed up his work, noting several recent improvements that enabled five men to stay down sixty feet for nearly two hours. Pointing out the practical uses of his bell and suit, he said they would be a great help in "Fishing for Pearl, Diving for Coral, Spunges and the like, in far greater Depths than has hitherto been possible. Also for the fitting and plaining of the foundations of Bridges upon Rocky Bottoms; and for the cleaning and scrubbing of Ships Bottoms when foul in calm Weather at Sea."

When Halley finished the salvage of the "Guiney frigat," he was not yet thirty-five. He lived half a century longer, proving much more hardy than the rulers of England: he outlasted Oliver and Richard Cromwell, Charles II, James II, William III, Queen Anne, and George I—and lived halfway through the reign of George II.

Although astronomy remained his major interest, his abundant curiosity led him into a multitude of other activities. In 1692 he compiled the first tables of mortality rates and thus became the virtual originator of the science of life statistics. Next, he was made Comptroller of the Mint at

Chester. This position was supposed to be merely honorary, a reward in the form of additional income for his scientific achievements. Halley, however, became so interested that he set about improving the alloy from which the coins were minted. In fact, his interest became so keen that the regular officials at the mint raised an uproar over what they regarded as interference, and after two years Halley resigned.

By 1698 his various achievements had brought him such fame that Czar Peter the Great, on a visit to England, came to him for advice about establishing a navy and introducing the sciences into Russia. The Czar, captivated by Halley's great good sense and high good humor, became his boon companion. One story is told that after an evening of carousing around London the Czar ordered Halley to trundle him home in a wheelbarrow. For once in his life Edmond Halley lost his sense of direction, and wheeled the ruler of Russia straight through a yew hedge.

Later that same year William III appointed Halley commander of the sloop of war, *Pink the Paramour*, for a voyage that was to combine exploration with scientific observation. He was to test his theory governing the magnetic needle in compasses, call at the English settlements in America and determine their latitudes and longitudes, and discover what he could about the lands that lay in the South Atlantic.

During his voyage he touched at St. Helena, the coast of Brazil, Cape Verde, the Barbados, Madeira, and the Canary Islands, among others. In the South Atlantic he "fell in with great islands of ice, of so incredible a height and magnitude that I scarce dare write my thoughts of it." During a stop at Bermuda, he observed a "Florida-Indian" diving naked after sponges. He noticed that the most experienced divers could stay down only a few minutes, even with what may have been the first of the self-contained underwater breathing apparatuses—a sponge dipped in oil to retain the air in its pores. The diver plunged, holding the sponge in his mouth. Then, when almost out of breath, he chewed on the sponge, releasing a small amount of air. Halley must certainly have felt a surge of pride in his diving suit then in use back in England.

The next year, again in command of *Pink the Paramour,* he observed the course of tides in the English Channel. As a result of this and his other voyages, he published a series of remarkably accurate maps and charts.

No undertaking seemed beyond the scope of his abilities. Queen Anne sent him on two missions to the Emperor of Germany to inspect harbors in the Adriatic and to help the imperial engineers fortify the harbor of Trieste. The Emperor was so pleased with the results that he drew a large diamond ring from his finger and gave it to Halley.

In 1705 Halley calculated the orbit of a comet that had streaked across the sky in 1682 and was to carry his name down through the centuries. When he predicted that it would reappear every seventy-six years, few believed him. Yet on Christmas Day, 1758, Halley's Comet again shot across the heavens and, true to his prediction, has continued its cycle ever since.

In 1719 he was given one of the highest honors that England could bestow upon her scientists—the appointment as Astronomer Royal at the Greenwich Observatory. There, although he was sixty-three years old, he set himself the task of observing the moon through a period of eighteen years— and carried it out. At eighty-one he suffered a slight paralysis of his right hand, but he kept right on, coming in to London every Thursday night to have dinner with his friends and attend the meetings of the Royal Society. Then, on the night of January 25, 1742, just a few months after his eighty-fifth birthday, he died.

History has placed Halley second only to Newton among the scientists of his time. But, as it has often been remarked, the world is much more likely to see another Isaac Newton than it is to see "this miracle of energy" that was Edmond Halley.

ROBERT FULTON

[1765–1815]

By JUNE, 1800, Paris was beginning to recover from the tumult of the French Revolution. Émigrés who had fled in terror seven years before were returning. Revolutionaries, grown prosperous, were moving into the great town-houses of the old aristocracy. Then, on June 14, Citizen Bonaparte won a great victory over the Austrians at the Battle of Marengo in the Italian Alps.

A few days later, while Paris still was celebrating Napoleon's triumph, a large crowd gathered on the banks of the Seine near the Hôtel des Invalides to watch an American engineer demonstrate his newest invention—a boat which he claimed could sink to the bottom of the river without drowning the crew and then rise again.

Among the crowd were several of Napoleon's agents; his curiosity had been aroused by this abrupt, eccentric Yankee who often called himself "Citizen Francis." The Connecticut poet Joel Barlow also was there, praying for the success of his countryman and friend, whom he had nicknamed "Toot."

"Citizen Francis"—or "Toot"—was thirty-four years old, a handsome, slender man six feet tall, with large dark eyes and curly brown hair. He looked like an artist, and he was one.

He also was a passionate republican, who fervently hoped that his new invention would prove the undoing of any navy —especially Britain's—that threatened the freedom of the seas. His real name was Robert Fulton.

At the time of the demonstration on the Seine, Robert Fulton had been away from America nearly fifteen years. Born November 14, 1765, on a farm in Little Britain, Lancaster County, Pennsylvania, he was named after his father, who died four years later, leaving his widow and five children practically penniless. At seventeen Robert went to seek his fortune in Philadelphia, where he gained some recognition as a painter of portraits and landscapes, as well as for his mechanical drawings. He also showed a knack for winning the friendship of influential citizens, among them Benjamin Franklin. In 1786, when Fulton was sent abroad to recover from lung trouble, Franklin gave him a letter of introduction to the American painter, Benjamin West, then having extraordinary success in London.

This first visit to England lasted eleven years. Like many young artists, Fulton complained of being almost "Crushed by Poverties Cold wind—and Freezing Rain." Actually the farm boy from Pennsylvania was clambering up the social ladder several rungs at a time, with considerable encouragement— financial as well as verbal—from Benjamin West, the Earl of Stanhope, the Duke of Bridgewater and many others. He spent the summer of 1791 at the castle of twenty-three-year-old Lord Courtenay, painting his host's portrait. The portrait was a success, and Fulton's patrons multiplied.

But by this time he was becoming more and more absorbed in engineering projects, and his painting became more a hobby than a vocation. By 1794 he had invented a device for raising and lowering boats in canals, a machine for sawing marble, another for spinning flax, and still another for twisting hemp rope. Two years later he published "A Treatise on the Improvement of Canal Navigation" and sent off a copy to George Washington. Fulton was making good, and he was proud of it. "He was fond," said one of his friends, "of being considered, as he really was, the maker of his own fortune."

Meanwhile, like Wordsworth and Coleridge and many another young man of that era, he had been excited and inspired by the dramatic events of the French Revolution. He had grown up in the midst of the American Revolution, and his thoughts now turned toward home. "I saw," he wrote, "that the growing wealth and commerce, and the increasing population of the United States, would compel them to look for a protection by sea, and perhaps drive them to the necessity of resorting to European measures, by establishing a navy. Seeing this, I turned my whole attention to find out means of destroying such engines of oppression, by some method which would put it out of the power of any nation to maintain such a system." The method he found was the *Nautilus*, first of a long line of famous submarines of the same name.

In 1797 he decided to return to America, by way of the France he so greatly admired. Immediately after reaching Paris in late June, he called on Joel Barlow and his wife. The Barlows were a middle-aged American couple, ardent supporters of the French Revolution, childless, socially prominent, and very wealthy. Soon Fulton had charmed them as completely as he had Franklin, West, and his various titled English friends. He moved into the Barlows' home as a guest —and stayed for seven years.

Shortly after their first meeting, "Toot" and Barlow were experimenting on the Seine with a machine to propel a torpedo-like device through the water. The results were disappointing, but Fulton was struck with a new idea. Immediately he wrote the French Directory proposing that he build "a mechanical Nautilus."

This notion of a submarine was not original with Fulton. Back in 1624 a Dutchman, Cornelius van Drebbel, had experimented with a submersible boat on the Thames; legend has it that King James I was a passenger on one of the tests. In 1776 David Bushnell, a Yale man, had built a submarine called the *Turtle* (because it looked like one), which made a unsuccessful attack on the British flagship, H.M.S. *Eagle*, in New York harbor. A number of other inventors had made tentative experiments, but up to Fulton's time no one had devised a practicable submarine.

When the French Directory showed interest, Fulton submitted a long list of demands, including a request for substantial payment, exclusive rights to the invention, a guarantee that the submarine not be used against America (unless America used it first!), and assurance that members of the crew would be given rank in the French Navy so that they could not be treated as pirates if captured by the English.

Hour after hour, day after day, for six long weeks Fulton impatiently paced the floors in the government offices, waiting for a decision. When word finally came rejecting his proposals, he sent a copy of his book on canals to Bonaparte, hoping to win the General's favor, and then submitted detailed plans for the *Nautilus* to the Minister of Marine. Turned down again, Fulton irately went to Holland in a futile attempt to interest the Dutch in his submarine.

When Napoleon became First Consul, however, Fulton rushed back to France. Apparently he was given encouragement by the government—and money by his friends—for by April of 1800, construction of the *Nautilus* was well under way at a boatyard in Rouen. She had a deck twenty feet long and six feet wide, with one mast and a fan-shaped sail for navigation on the surface. When the boat was about to submerge, the mast could be collapsed in two minutes. Beneath the cucumber-shaped hull, which was slightly longer than the deck, was a hollow keel, to be flooded by hand-operated pumps for the plunge. A rudder directed the craft up or down, and motion underwater was achieved by a hand-operated screw propeller.

For attacking enemy ships, the *Nautilus* had a detachable vertical spike on the conning tower. A mine trailed from a cord running through a hole in the spike. Once the spike had been detached and driven into the bottom of the enemy ship, the *Nautilus*, still pulling the cord, would move away, drawing the mine up tight against the target. There—so Fulton hoped —it would explode.

At last the day in mid-June arrived when the *Nautilus* was to be tested in public on the Seine. Fulton, as the craft's skipper, was risking his reputation, his life and the faith of his wealthy friends. With two daring crewmen, he climbed down into the odd-looking boat and closed the hatch behind him. The *Nautilus* plunged down into the Seine, and the crowd lining the banks waited in suspense. At last, after forty-five minutes underwater, the plunging boat broke the surface. Fulton had made good his claims.

Further tests of the *Nautilus* were made during the summer at Rouen and Havre and, elated with their success, Fulton returned to Paris. There Barlow listened with enthusiasm to his plans for improving the underwater vessel the following spring. Other influential friends arranged for an audience with Napoleon. Although no record has survived of this single meeting between the world-conquering Corsican and the ambitious farm boy from Pennsylvania, we do know that Napoleon ordered a commission to examine the merits of Fulton's submarine and then authorized further work.

In the spring of 1801 the *Nautilus* was transported to Brest. Fulton arrived to find she had become badly rusted during the winter, but by July she was cleaned up, repaired, improved, and ready for further tests.

Using three crewmen now, instead of two, Fulton embarked on a new series of tests in the harbor of Brest. He took the *Nautilus* down to twenty-five feet and remained there for an hour, refusing to go deeper for fear greater pressure might crush the boat. Finding that candles consumed too much air, he had a glass window installed near the bow. Nine inches thick but only an inch-and-a-half in diameter, it gave enough light twenty-five feet underwater for him to count the minutes on his watch. Further tests showed that the *Nautilus* could be steered by a compass and that she could circle back to her starting point. Even more important, while submerged she could cover nearly 1,500 feet in seven minutes. Later, carrying a copper globe containing compressed air, Fulton and his crew of three stayed underwater for six hours.

On one hot July day Fulton hoisted the sail, to see how the *Nautilus* would act on the surface. With only a light breeze, the boat moved scarcely two miles an hour, but she tacked as well as any traditional sailing boat.

Important as these tests were, they were not dramatic enough to excite the French government. So Fulton arranged for something more colorful. As an important French admiral and a horde of spectators watched, the *Nautilus*, trailing a mine containing twenty pounds of powder, approached a small boat anchored in the harbor at Brest. A few seconds later the mine struck the boat and exploded, blowing a column of water and fragments from 80 to 100 feet in the air.

In early September he tried something even more daring—to track down and blow up some of the British ships then blockading the French coast. Twice, just as he came within sight of the enemy, the ships hoisted sail and moved swiftly away, having been forewarned by spies that Fulton and his strange craft were on the prowl. Then, as winter drew nearer, heavy gales arose, and the forays had to be ended. Even though "Citizen Francis" had not managed to sink the British Navy, he had demonstrated that the *Nautilus* could make a voyage of more than seventy miles on the high seas.

When Napoleon asked to examine the underwater boat, Fulton wrote that he had already dismantled the *Nautilus* and sold the pieces for scrap. His ardor for the French cause had been diminishing steadily, and he was taking no chances that his plans or his boat might be seized—or stolen. For their part, the French had little time for Fulton after his failure to destroy even one British ship. Napoleon was quoted as calling Fulton a charlatan. "Toot" retaliated by saying that the Corsican should be "hunted down as the enemy of mankind."

Meanwhile, the new American Minister had just arrived in France—the wealthy, ingenious Robert R. Livingston. Fulton made it a point to meet him, and soon they had signed an agreement to build a steamboat which—so they hoped—would be much more practicable than any of the experimental steamboats previously built. By the spring of 1803 their first boat was ready. Before it could be tested, however, a frantic messenger burst into Fulton's quarters shouting, "Oh, sir, the boat has broken in pieces, and gone to the bottom!" He spoke the truth; the machinery was so heavy it had crashed through the frame. Undaunted, a new, and stronger, boat was made ready by July. Its test on the Seine was a success.

Now, a year-and-a-half after the last of Fulton's underwater experiments, the British suddenly grew alarmed about this threat to their naval supremacy. Fulton did his part in arousing this furor by writing his friend, the Earl of Stanhope, about his tests; the Earl promptly made a fiery speech in the House of Lords. Fulton—no doubt as he expected—soon received an offer to come build a submarine for the British.

By May of 1804 "Citizen Francis" was in London, having been promised a salary of £200 a month and reimbursement for all expenses in constructing his devices. William Pitt, now Prime Minister, was deeply interested, but others fiercely opposed the American engineer's radical schemes. The First Lord of the Admiralty raged that "Pitt was the greatest fool that ever existed, to encourage a mode of warfare which those who commanded the seas did not want and which, if successful, would deprive them of it." Fulton's plans, however, show that his English submarine—which was never built—would have been far superior to the *Nautilus*.

He did direct several tests with floating mines, which he called torpedoes, but an expensive expedition against the Boulogne flotilla and another against the ships in Calais harbor in October of 1804 resulted only in the destruction of one light sailing ship and its crew of twenty-one.

The next fall Fulton arranged a demonstration near Deal within a mile of Walmar Castle, the residence of Pitt. In a letter Fulton wrote: "Yesterday, about 4 o'clock, I made the intended experiment on the brig, with a carcass of 170 pounds of powder . . . Exactly in 15 minutes from the time of drawing the peg, and throwing the carcass into the water, the explosion took place. It lifted the brig almost bodily, and broke her completely in two . . . At the time of her going up, she did not appear to make more resistance than a bag of feathers, and went to pieces like a shattered egg-shell."

Less than a week later—on October 21, 1805—Lord Nelson won his great victory over the combined French and Spanish fleets at Trafalgar, and the English had no further need of Fulton. A year later he embarked for his native land, which he had left two decades earlier. Just before sailing, he wrote to Joel Barlow, already back in America, to have a roast goose ready to celebrate his return.

As it turned out, "Toot" had good reason to celebrate. Within eight months of his return, the *Clermont*—the first commercially practicable steamboat—had been built and had made her historic trip up the Hudson to Albany and back to New York City. In partnership with Robert Livingston, Fulton found himself at the head of a thriving steamboat company (and eventually he built the first steam-propelled warship). Within five more months he had married Livingston's second cousin, Harriet, beautiful, charming, witty and wealthy. She bore him five children.

His interest in submarines and mines did not flag. In July of 1807, authorized by the government, he prepared to blow up a large hulk brig in New York harbor. Several unsuccessful attempts were made to place and fire the mines. The large crowd of spectators grew more and more impatient. Finally the explosion took place: nothing was seen of the vessel but a high column of smoke, water and fragments.

Early in 1810 he visited the city of Washington to interest Jefferson and Madison in his projects, and in March Congress granted him $5,000. That fall, as a demonstration, he tried to blow up an abandoned sloop of war, the *Argus*, but a wily navy commodore surrounded the sloop with cables and foiled Fulton's attempts. Two years later he designed an underwater gun to fire a harpoon with a cord trailing a mine; the mine would then float against the side of the boat and explode.

Fulton's very last project, a new version of his submarine, was a boat slightly over eighty feet long, carrying a crew of 100 men, designed to submerge only deep enough to leave the deck level with the surface. Before this boat, the *Mute,* could be completed, Fulton was stricken with pneumonia. He died on February 24, 1815, just four months before Napoleon's defeat at the Battle of Waterloo. Ironically, it is the *Clermont* —an immediate commercial success—for which Robert Fulton is remembered. To him it was a mere side issue to his beloved and ingenious submarines, for which the world was not yet ready.

WILHELM BAUER

[1822–1875]

Few chapters in the history of underwater pioneers are as colorful—or as ill-fated—as the life of Wilhelm Sebastian Valentin Bauer. Born on December 23, 1822, in the small village of Dillingen, near Augsburg, Bavaria—a country with no seacoast and no navy—he devoted his life to building an underwater boat.

His father, a blunt, hard-headed, unimaginative man, was a corporal in the Bavarian army. Raised amid the rough, devil-may-care atmosphere of an army post, apprenticed at thirteen to a brutal carpenter, young Wilhelm had his first taste of freedom when he reached seventeen and, according to custom, was allowed to set out on the road to practice his craft. His travels led him north to the ports of Bremen, Hamburg and Lübeck, where he was fascinated by his first sight of ships and the sea. Bursting with the spirit of adventure, he planned to travel on to the Orient. Instead, his father—determined that Wilhelm should not become a dreamy vagabond—forced him to enlist in the Bavarian army.

Fiercely resentful, Bauer nevertheless became a good soldier and an expert fencer and horseman, but his happiest moments were spent sketching the carved ornaments which decorated the old monastery in Augsburg where the troops were quartered. Then, with money earned from giving riding and fencing lessons, he bribed the sergeant-major to let him set up a workshop in a corner of the monastery cellar. There he invented one gadget after another.

In 1848 war flared between Denmark and the German Confederation over Schleswig-Holstein, a small state on the border. Bavaria, a member of the Confederation, sent its troops to the front, including Bauer's artillery regiment. During one battle the Danes were holding a bridge. All attempts to dislodge them proved futile. If only some way could be found, thought Bauer, to approach the bridge underwater and blow it up, and the Danes along with it. A few days later, down on the coast, he noticed the ease with which a seal moved through the water. Here was the ideal shape for his underwater boat!

Rushing back to camp, he resigned from the Bavarian army and re-enlisted in the Schleswig-Holstein forces, where he hoped to interest the navy in his plans. In a few weeks he had a working model ready. At a demonstration in Kiel harbor, the miniature boat, operated by a clockwork mechanism, moved ahead underwater for five minutes. Although impressed, the naval officers declared they had no funds to build a full-scale boat.

Bauer became furious when the men who had loaned him money for the project demanded the model as payment. In a rage, he grabbed a sledge hammer and smashed the model to pieces. All they had paid for, he said, was the material, and that was all they should have.

The hot-headed Bavarian was immediately transferred. His new commanding general, impressed by the intense young soldier, collected enough money from the troops to finance the building of the submarine. But government officials, resentful of a foreigner and suspicious of any innovation, meddled constantly. Cut costs, they said. Make the sides lighter. Omit the two cylinders to hold the water and pig-iron ballast; the keel has enough space for the ballast. Rather than abandon his dream, Bauer gave in to their demands.

The finished boat, propelled by two hand-operated tread-wheels, was slightly less than twenty-five feet long, ten feet high, and six feet wide. The keel would be flooded to submerge, and a heavy weight could be moved forward to make the nose dip, then moved back to keep the boat at a given depth. Two pumps were installed to force the water out. Outside, but operated from within, was an arm to attach an explosive charge to the bottom of an enemy ship.

Bauer undertook the first test alone, on a moonlit night in December of 1850. In fourteen minutes the boat traveled about two-and-a-half miles under the waters of Kiel harbor and, quite by accident, achieved a significant military victory. The Danes blockading the harbor heard through their spies that a strange sea demon was about to attack. In a panic, they hauled up anchor and sailed away to the north.

Even with a one-man crew, the *Sea Demon*, as Bauer immediately christened her, showed an alarming tendency to sink deeper than planned. Ignoring his warnings that the cheaply built boat was unseaworthy, the authorities insisted on more extensive tests. So, in February, his will drawn up and signed, Bauer and a crew of two, Witt and Thomsen, boarded the boat at nine in the morning, closed the hatch, and moved out toward the deepest part of the harbor. A crowd of curiosity seekers and skeptical officials lined the shore and overflowed into rowboats dotting the water.

The cocks were opened, water poured in, and the boat began to sink. Suddenly the stern dipped, and the loosely stowed iron ballast rolled aft, threatening to shatter the boat's thin shell. Down she went, sinking almost perpendicularly, to twenty-eight, twenty-nine, thirty feet. "She hasn't broken apart yet," shouted Bauer. "We still have a chance!"

Scarcely were the words out of his mouth when part of the left treadwheel snapped off. Then an oak beam on the right side splintered; rivets were loosened; water seeped in. Faster and faster the *Sea Demon* hurtled downward. Then the stern struck bottom, fifty-two feet down. Slowly the boat settled to a horizontal position.

Bauer tried to encourage his crew. If enough water seeped in to compress the air and build up the pressure inside to equal the pressure of the water outside, then, he said, they could force open the hatch and escape.

But Witt and Thomsen, standing in ice-cold water up to their chests, refused to listen. Desperately they manned the half-disabled pumps while Bauer, wrapped in his military cloak, stood silently watching. Finally, afraid they would be too exhausted to swim when the moment came to escape, Bauer opened the cocks wide, and water poured in.

Aghast, Witt and Thomsen begged him not to hasten their death. Then Thomsen, crazed by fear, came at him with a knife, but the sight of Bauer's service revolver stopped the frenzied sailor in his tracks. The revolver was thoroughly wet and would not fire, yet it had served to quell the first underwater mutiny.

By eleven o'clock the rescuers above managed to locate the sunken *Sea Demon*. At two-thirty they dropped chains, hoping to snare the wreck and lift it. The three men below trembled as the chains banged against the boat, threatening to stave in the already weakened sides and release the precious air pressure that had been built up. To the immense relief of

Bauer and his crew, the rescue attempts were at last abandoned.

Witt, strongest of the three in the *Sea Demon*, now tried to raise the hatch. It gave way, but, terrified by the onrush of water, he let it snap closed. Bauer urged him on. Success! Bauer grabbed the half-fainting Thomsen by the hair and dragged him through the hatchway after Witt. The column of escaping air hurled all three men upward like corks popping from champagne bottles—the first recorded free escape from a submarine. It was now four-thirty in the afternoon; they had been trapped below for seven-and-a-half hours.

Bauer, Witt and Thomsen bobbed up on the surface right in the middle of the funeral service being conducted for them. At first the mourners were dumbfounded, and then a roar of relief echoed round the shore.

In the hard months that followed, Bauer refused to admit defeat. Mustered out of the army when the war ended, he became a vagabond, but with a purpose: to gain backing for a new submarine. Gradually he scraped together enough money to build a new working model. A trip to Trieste to interest the Austrian naval authorities in his project proved futile.

Then his hopes soared. From Osborne on the Isle of Wight came a summons to visit Queen Victoria and Prince Albert. A native German himself, Albert was highly sympathetic. One day he suggested that Bauer wind up the clockwork mechanism and send the model on a dive under the royal yacht and up on the other side. With a cord attached to the little boat to haul it back to safety, what was there to lose? Everything, as it turned out. The seas were rough; the cord parted; and Bauer's highly prized model dived straight down to a watery grave.

Bauer was heartbroken. Albert supplied money for another

model, but, ironically, his support hurt more than it helped. The members of the Admiralty always resented the German-born prince's meddling in their affairs, and here he was trying to aid another German! Months passed as the naval officers resorted to one delaying tactic after another. Bauer grew more impatient and more embittered.

Then, in 1854, the French lured him to Paris to demonstrate his model. The discussion of his proposals was deliberately drawn out so that the meeting had to be adjourned to a second day. Assured that the precious model would be perfectly safe, Bauer was persuaded to leave it in the conference room. The moment he entered the room the next morning he saw that his invention had been tampered with; someone had broken several parts trying to discover how it worked. Tucking the model under his arm, he stalked out of the building. Refusing to have any further dealings with the French, he returned to London, where an Englishman swindled him much more effectively.

This was a man named John Scott Russell, who, among other speculations, owned a large dockyard. Bauer signed a contract to let Scott Russell build his submarine in return for two-thirds of the profits. At the end of seven months, construction had not even begun. Instead, Scott Russell severed relations with Bauer, saying he planned to build a submarine of his own invention. Bauer, convinced that his designs had been stolen, went to the law—only to learn that the contract had been a sham and that he had no recourse whatsoever.

Violent quarrels followed with Scott Russell, with the Admiralty, with practically everyone but Prince Albert. In one argument Bauer announced he would build his submarine for the Russians, whom England then was battling in the Crimea. A British admiral, in turn, threatened to hang Bauer from the highest mast in the fleet. Bauer retorted that his submarine would sink the ship as deep as they had planned to hang him high!

One evening when Bauer returned to his lodgings, he learned that orders had been issued to seize his model and plans if he attempted to leave England. That very night he rented a small fishing boat and, under cover of darkness, loaded it with his possessions. At two in the morning he rowed down the Thames to the spot where a steamer bound for Hamburg was anchored. Like a hunted criminal, he fled the land to which he had come with such high hopes. He had only one consolation: the submarine Scott Russell built sank on one of its first trials.

Bauer carried out his threat of going to Russia and, at the invitation of Grand Duke Konstantine, arrived in St. Petersburg in May, 1855. Again, as a foreigner of lowly birth, Bauer met with hostility, but Konstantine was a forceful (and sometimes frightening) supporter. By November a new submarine —the *Fire Diver*—was finished: fifty-two feet long, twelve-and-a-half feet high, eleven feet wide, with sides of forged iron one-half inch thick, supported by iron ribs three-and-a-half inches thick. Operated by manpower, the *Fire Diver* had strong pumps, three large cylinders to hold the water ballast, five windows in the top and sixteen in the sides and on the bottom.

Bauer marshalled 200 sailors to haul the machine from the shipyard to the banks of the Neva River. From there the Russian Navy was to transport her to Kronstadt. For seven months the *Fire Diver* sat there while the Navy filibustered, warning that the weird contraption was sure to sink and block the shipping lanes of the Neva.

One of the most active conspirators against Bauer was Fedorowitsch, the Russian lieutenant in charge of the *Fire Diver*'s crew. Resentful at being placed at the service of a former enlisted man—and a Bavarian as well—Fedorowitsch was in an ideal spot to sabotage Bauer's plans.

Bauer made good use of the delay by training his crew to use the diving chamber he had built in the *Fire Diver*. But finally he became so exasperated that he persuaded Konstantine to give him full authority to have the boat moved. To thwart him, the Navy loaded the *Fire Diver* on a barge and pointed out that the cargo sat too high to pass under the bridge spanning the Neva. Bauer's answer was to take an axe and hack a hole in the barge so big that it sank, leaving the *Fire Diver* floating. Hitching the submarine to a tugboat, Bauer and his crew set out for Kronstadt.

As they came down the river toward the port, Bauer cast off from the tug so that the *Fire Diver* could enter the harbor under her own power. The crew was below and only about five feet of the boat showed above the surface. "Halt or be shot!" shouted the terrified sentry. It was too late: the *Fire Diver* broke through the barrier supposedly protecting the harbor. At three in the morning of May 26, 1856, Bauer, triumphantly astride his invention, entered Kronstadt harbor.

After a fews hours' rest Bauer was eager to test the boat's ability to submerge. His crew, however, had long since declared they would not dive until the Pope had blessed the venture. Impatient to get started, Bauer said he planned only to take on some water ballast to see whether the *Fire Diver* could maintain her balance. The hatch was closed, the cocks opened. Suddenly the sailors were terrified to see water creeping up past the windows. They had been tricked! Frantically they manned the pumps, and when the windows finally rose above the water again, they tossed their caps in the air, shouting for joy.

All through the summer of 1856 Bauer experimented. He found the air supply would last his crew of eleven for seven hours and that in calm waters they had plenty of light to steer toward an objective. With primitive equipment, he took what were probably the first underwater photographs. Fully aware of his own poor education, Bauer implored Russian scientists to board his submarine to study the underwater world, but they haughtily refused.

On September 6, 1856, the gala coronation of Czar Alexander II took place in Moscow. In Kronstadt, Bauer held his own festivities. At nine in the morning he took four navy trumpeters aboard, submerged, and as the first salute was fired from the fortress, the strains of the Russian national anthem echoed from the deep, where Bauer was conducting the first underwater concert in history. Within the *Fire Diver* the trumpeters found that their instruments gave forth a much lighter tone than in the open air. This concert, which could be heard nearly 750 feet from where the boat was submerged, lasted till one o'clock, when a big salvo from the assembled Russian fleet announced that the coronation was over.

But Bauer's enemies told Konstantine that the Bavarian had followed the national anthem with an Hungarian revolutionary march, turning the whole event into an anti-government political demonstration. Hearing of this, Bauer was terrified; he had been in Russia long enough to know how easy it was to be exiled to Siberia. It took him many anxious weeks to dispel Konstantine's suspicions.

Having conducted 133 successful dives, Bauer now was eager to increase the *Fire Diver*'s speed—and her tactical

effectiveness—by installing an engine. His enemies finally succeeded in defeating the iron-willed Bavarian, however. He
was ordered to demonstrate the combat possibilities of the
Fire Diver by blowing up a large old ship riding at anchor in
Kronstadt harbor. The day before the demonstration, Lieutenant Fedorowitsch deliberately had the ship towed to a spot
so shallow the *Fire Diver* could not pass beneath it. Scarcely
200 feet from the ship Bauer realized he had been betrayed.
Then something happened that not even Lieutenant Fedorowitsch had bargained for. The *Fire Diver* grazed bottom, and
her screw propeller became entangled in the rigging of an
ancient wreck.

No equipment for divers was on board. Bauer ordered the
iron ballast discarded and the water pumped out—all to no
avail. Finally the boat tilted upward, so that the hatch was
just a bit below the surface. Fedorowitsch immediately opened
the hatch, clambered out, and swam to one of the small rowboats clustered nearby, carrying observers.

Bauer was unable to close the hatch. Wave after wave
poured in. At last there was no alternative: Bauer ordered
the sailors to abandon ship. On its 134th dive, the *Fire Diver*
had come to disaster.

Bauer lost no time in rushing to St. Petersburg to reveal the
sabotage to Konstantine. Fedorowitsch was severely punished;
the naval authorities were ordered to salvage the *Fire Diver*
at once; and Bauer was made an imperial submarine engineer,
with the rank of major.

But the Russian Navy was not to be crossed. From all sides
Bauer was subjected to such harrassment that finally, in utter
despair, he resigned. As compensation, he was given the *Fire
Diver*, but prohibited from taking her out of Russia. After
selling the boat for a fraction of her worth, he left Russia

in the spring of 1858 with only one thing of value: his wife, Sophie Hösly, the daughter of a German foreman in the St. Petersburg shipyard where the *Fire Diver* had been built.

One misfortune after another followed his departure from Russia at the age of thirty-five. The King of Bavaria planned to reward him with a state position—until it was disclosed that Bauer had once been a lowly enlisted man. Bauer designed a flying machine, but it was never built. A second trip to England, in 1860, served only to increase his debts. A trip to Trieste the same year proved futile. From 1861 to 1863 he succeeded in salvaging a steamer sunk in Lake Constance— a moral victory only, for his reward scarcely covered his expenses.

Then the Austro-Prussian War flared up, and in the tumult Wilhelm Bauer was forgotten. One after the other, his two small sons and his little daughter died. In 1869 illness forced him to take to his bed. Through the efforts of his wife and a journalist who admired his achievements, the state finally granted him a tiny pension which helped a bit to alleviate the poverty of his last few years. Paralyzed, speechless, almost forgotten by the world, Wilhelm Bauer died on June 18, 1875, at the age of only fifty-two.

SIMON LAKE

[1866-1945]

THIS BOAT CRAWLS
ALONG THE BOTTOM

At Least That's What It Was to
Do, but It Escapes and Aston-
ishes Folks in Oceanic, N.J.

FUN FOR MERRY MERMEN

The *New York Herald* had quite a story to tell on January 9, 1895. Two days before, the young son of a minister in
Oceanic, New Jersey, had slipped out of the house at dawn
to go duck hunting on the banks of the Shrewsbury River.
Suddenly he stumbled on what seemed to be a three-wheeled
coffin, with *Argonaut, Jr.* painted on the side. Quick as a
flash he dashed home to spread the news.

The next morning, as a crowd examined the weird object,
a rowboat pulled in to shore. Out stepped stocky, twenty-
eight-year-old Simon Lake. The *Argonaut, Jr.*, he announced,
was his first submarine. Designed to crawl on her wheels along
the bottom "five miles without coming up to breathe," she

had instead floated away on the surface during a strong gale on Christmas night. This was not the last time Simon Lake and his submarines were to make headlines.

Simon Lake had been born on September 4, 1866, in Pleasantville, New Jersey, into a family of mechanical geniuses and business failures. His grandfather had invented a seed-planter, his uncle a whistling buoy and an improved mowing machine, his father the shade roller for windows. Not one of them had managed to hold on to what little money he made. Blunt, brilliant, red-headed Simon Lake upheld the family tradition.

At ten he had discovered the wonders of Jules Verne's *Twenty Thousand Leagues Under the Sea*, and from that time on he was determined to set out on underwater voyages to rival those of Verne's fictional hero, Captain Nemo. Before he was fourteen he had drawn up plans for a submarine which, like most of those he later designed, was intended not for warfare, but for salvage, treasure hunting and scientific exploration.

During his 1882 summer vacation from boarding school—the Clinton Liberal Institute in Fort Plain, New York—young Simon undertook his first underwater adventure, on the Toms River in New Jersey. Having read about the use of diving bells, he dragged his flimsy homemade canvas canoe down to the river, flipped the craft upside down, and dived beneath, to see how long the air trapped within would last him. Local fishermen, spotting the drifting canoe, raised the alarm that the crazy Lake youngster had been drowned. When Simon appeared, breathless but safe, he barely escaped a whipping.

Through with school at seventeen, Simon Lake became a full-fledged inventor in the next ten years, with patents on an improved steering gear for high-wheel bicycles (later adapted for use on small boats), a safety winch, and a capping machine, among others. Now living in Baltimore, he worked from early in the morning until well after midnight, week after week, heartily encouraged by his wife, Margaret, whom he had married in 1890. A small manufacturing company he had founded was on the verge of flourishing when he discovered that his backers were unethical. Always a man of passionate, unimpeachable honesty, he closed down the business immediately.

He then turned his energies to revising and perfecting his plans for a submarine. One night he came home to find his wife greatly excited by news that the Navy was advertising for bids on a submarine. When she urged him to enter the competition, Lake hesitated—at only twenty-six, with no reputation and no influential backers, what chance would he have?

Nevertheless, in June, 1893, Simon Lake appeared at the navy offices in Washington, to find the rooms crowded with politicians, lawyers and lobbyists. The unworldly young inventor was relieved that only two others had come with plans for submarines. One was George F. Baker, who had experimented with an underwater boat the year before. The other was John P. Holland.

Holland was then fifty-two, twice Lake's age. As early as 1875 he had proposed a submarine to the Navy. Then, with private funds, he built a submarine which failed on its trials, but won him the backing of the Fenian Brotherhood, fiery Irish patriots determined to oust the English from Ireland. His second submarine, dubbed the *Fenian Ram* by the newspapers, was catapulted into international notoriety in 1883 when the Fenians kidnapped her in New York and sailed up to New Haven. There they navigated the *Ram* so hazardously that shipping authorities finally banned her from the water, and she was hauled up on shore and abandoned. By 1893, however, Holland had won the support of a reputable, if ruthless, financier who commanded a large group of lobbyists in Congress.

Holland's plans—which called for a submarine that would submerge head first in a series of short, jerky dives—were selected by the Navy. Simon Lake raged when he heard the decision. His own plans, he felt, contained significant innovations. They provided for the crew's comfort and stressed the vessel's capabilities on the surface as well as underwater. Most important of all, his submarine would be the first in history to submerge smoothly, on an even keel (a principle soon to be followed throughout the world), by flooding her tanks and then controlling her stability underwater with a fin-like arrangement called hydroplanes. In his mind Lake christened his wheeled boat the *Argonaut*, after the legendary Greek sailors who sought the golden fleece.

For six futile months in New York Lake tried to raise funds to build his *Argonaut*. Then he moved to his aunt's home in Atlantic Highlands, New Jersey, and began to scrape together materials to build a small version of the *Argonaut* with his own hands. This was the *Argonaut, Jr.,* the floating coffin which caused such a stir that January morning in 1895. Fourteen feet long, five feet high, flat-sided and flat-bottomed, with two wheels forward and one aft, the craft was made of double layers of pine planking interlined with canvas. An old hand pump and a tank from a bankrupt soda fountain provided the compressed air. A crude hand-crank operated the propeller.

Lake was especially proud of her forward chamber, the air lock. When the door to the submarine proper was closed and the air pressure in the chamber raised to equal the water pressure outside, then a door in the bottom could be opened without danger: the air pressure would keep the water from entering. Wearing a homemade diving helmet he had hammered out of iron, Lake could step from his submarine to the bottom of the Shrewsbury River or New York Bay to pick up clams and oysters or to spear fish.

The little *Argonaut, Jr.* attracted so much attention that Simon Lake soon was able to raise enough funds to build his full-scale *Argonaut*. Both she and the *Plunger*, the submarine Holland had designed for the Navy, were built in the same Baltimore works and launched the same month—August of 1897. The *Plunger* was a failure, but the *Argonaut* had a thrilling and eventful life.

Thirty-seven feet long, equipped with wheels and an air lock, the *Argonaut* was the first submarine ever to operate successfully with a gasoline engine. Had the Navy not been so determined to oppose Lake, the *Argonaut* might have proved a valuable weapon in the Spanish-American War, which had just broken out. Nosing around Hampton Roads, she ferreted out every one of the mines the Navy had planted. Still the admirals were unimpressed. The Cuban Junta, however, sought to buy the ship as a mine-layer. When their agent boarded the *Argonaut* for a demonstration, Lake proudly conducted his visitor into the air lock. As air began to hiss into the chamber, the agent became hysterical, screaming that Lake was trying to assassinate him. When the *Argonaut* surfaced, the Cuban fled. Simon Lake never heard from the Junta again.

Lake experimented constantly. For the air supply he first attached hoses to buoys on the surface; later, for greater mobility, he designed mast-like pipes, reaching to the surface, which enabled the *Argonaut* to move freely at depths up to fifty feet. In January, 1898, he established an underwater telephone station on the boat and talked while submerged in the

Chesapeake with Baltimore, Washington and New York. That summer he took two blurred, indistinct pictures of fish peering through the forward window. Apparently he was unaware that Louis Boutan, a French zoologist, had achieved considerable success with underwater photography as early as 1893. Boutan, equipped with a camera in a watertight case, had actually descended in a diving suit to take his pictures. Some of them appeared in *The Century Magazine* for May, 1898, eight months before Simon Lake's efforts were published in *McClure's*.

The *Argonaut*'s most dramatic exploit took place in the fall of 1898, on her first run from Baltimore to New York, a daring venture even in calm seas. Caught by a severe nor'easter in which more than 200 ships were lost, Lake had himself lashed outside the conning tower to direct the *Argonaut*. By the time Sandy Hook—and safety—were reached at three in the morning, he was practically encased in ice from head to toe.

The perilous voyage had taught him that the cigar-shaped structure of the *Argonaut* was not buoyant enough to rise with rough seas. Taking her to Brooklyn, he cut her in half and added both a twenty-foot mid-section and a ship-shaped superstructure. Afloat, the *Argonaut* now resembled a graceful yacht.

Lacking powerful financial backing, Lake tried to get all the free publicity he could. In Baltimore, soon after launching the *Argonaut*, he had invited twenty-three journalists (including one intrepid woman) aboard for a trial dive in Chesapeake Bay. Two of the reporters provided champagne, served in the boat's rusty cup. The underwater party made good newspaper copy. So did a frightened fisherman a few weeks later who claimed to have seen the devil, wearing a red cap, rise from the sea—it was red-headed Simon Lake, emerging from the hatch after the *Argonaut* had surfaced. In Bridgeport, Connecticut, where he moved his operations in 1899, Lake invited twenty-seven of the town's elite for a trip on the bottom of Long Island Sound. Once submerged, they sang songs, picked up clams through the door in the air lock, and ate a savory fish dinner cooked underwater. Completely oblivious to the passage of time, the party arrived back in Bridgeport at four in the afternoon, two hours overdue, to find the docks crowded with mourning relatives and friends who had concluded that all aboard the *Argonaut* had perished.

One day, while working in his Bridgeport office, Lake accidentally discovered the right combination of prisms and lenses for a periscope, but before the combination was written down, a clumsy office boy jumbled the lenses. Fortunately, when Lake explained to a professor at Johns Hopkins what he had done, the professor was able to work out the optical principle involved. Soon Lake submarines were equipped with workable periscopes.

His determination to interest the United States government in his invention never wavered. Having formed the Lake Torpedo Boat Company, he built a new submarine in 1901, the sixty-five-foot *Protector*, and persuaded Secretary of War William Howard Taft to appoint an Army board to examine her potential for coastal defense. On her official trials the *Protector* performed splendidly, laying mines, cutting cables, and even breaking through eight inches of ice on Narragansett Bay with great ease. As a result, the Army had a bill introduced into the Senate for the purchase of five Lake submarines; navy lobbyists caused its defeat.

Then came the Russo-Japanese War. Foreign agents were reported lurking around Lake's shipyard in Bridgeport. Lake denied any negotiations were under way. On June 10, 1904, the story exploded into headlines in *The New York Times:*

SUBMARINE BOAT ABOARD AND BOUND FOR JAPAN?

Incoming Skipper Saw Queer Deckload on the Fortuna

COAL FOR CORK? GUESS NOT

The Submarine Craft Protector Disappeared from Bridgeport After Being Examined by Japanese Officers

Ostensibly bound for Cork with a cargo of coal, the steamer *Fortuna* had sailed from Norfolk. However, on Sunday morning, June 5, despite a thick haze covering the water, observers had seen her lying off Sandy Hook, with a floating derrick standing by. Meanwhile, the *Protector* had disappeared on a run out of Bridgeport. Then the captain of an incoming Norwegian ship reported that he had passed the *Fortuna*, outward bound, with a canvas-covered object on her deck that looked more like a submarine than a cargo of coal.

On June 15 Simon Lake sailed on a passenger ship, still refusing to comment on the mysterious disappearance of the *Protector*. Everyone realized the reason for secrecy: with the United States a neutral, if the *Protector* had been sold to Japan she would have been seized as contraband of war. There was considerable surprise when the *Protector* turned up in Kronstadt harbor. She had been bought by Russia—not Japan—for $250,000.

Except for a few brief trips back to the United States, Simon Lake spent seven years abroad. The *Protector* (which ultimately was stationed in the harbor at Vladivostok) performed so well that the Russians commissioned Lake to build eleven more submarines. Lake expanded his organization, opening offices in Germany, Italy, Austria and England.

Despite the money he was making, Simon Lake—even after his family joined him—was not happy away from home. He was shocked by the immorality of the Russian aristocrats and by the stupidity of the Russian officers. One time, for example, out in the Gulf of Finland, the *Protector* was moving with only her conning tower awash. Lake went out to watch a school of fish. Suddenly he realized that the boat was submerging. Leaping inside, he closed the hatch with only a moment to spare. There, roaring with laughter, was the senior Russian officer, delighted with the scare he had given Lake and totally unaware how near he had brought the *Protector* and her crew to disaster. Finally both Simon Lake and his wife decided that Russia was not the place in which to raise their three children. They moved to Germany and then to England.

Here, Lake's interest in using the submarine for salvage revived. At the turn of the century back in Bridgeport he had developed a cylindrical cargo-carrier which could be submerged, loaded with salvage, and floated back to the surface. He had also devised a tremendous tube large enough for a diver to crawl through, which could be lowered from a boat into the water. At the lower end was an observation chamber, similar to his submarine air lock. Now, in England, he built another such tube to undertake the salvage of the *Lutine*, which had gone to the bottom of the Zuider Zee in 1799 with six million dollars worth of gold aboard. Just as the salvage operation was about to start, he heard that a new bill for his submarines was before Congress. He and his family immediately sailed for home.

At last Lake submarines saw service with the United States Navy. In 1912 he built the *Seal* and in 1912 the *Tuna;* soon a number of others were commissioned, including the *S-48*.

During World War I he tried in vain to interest the government in using submarines as cargo-carriers. The Germans, however, appropriated his ideas for their successful cargo-carrying submarine, the *Deutschland*.

After World War I Lake met with one financial disaster after another. His European business died out as country after country infringed on his patents. A company he founded to manufacture concrete blocks went bankrupt; Lake personally assumed all obligations, selling the Lake Torpedo Boat Company to make good the debts.

One of Lake's greatest disappointments occurred in 1931. Sir Hubert Wilkins, the Australian explorer, planned to sail directly to the North Pole under the Arctic ice. For this expedition Lake designed a new superstructure for the Navy's *O-12* and added a diving compartment so that scientists could collect Arctic marine life and samples of polar mud through the open door. Flaws in the engine and electric equipment prevented the submarine—renamed the *Nautilus*—from completing her mission, and she eventually was scuttled in a Norwegian fjord. However, some valuable oceanographic information had been obtained by the scientists aboard, one of whom was Harald Ulrik Sverdrup, the eminent Norwegian who later became director of the Scripps Institution of Oceanography at La Jolla, California.

Lake's misfortunes continued. Later that same year he announced that he planned to use the *Lutine* salvage tube to recover the purser's safe from the *Lusitania*, the luxury liner torpedoed by the Germans in 1915. The job, he said, should take only two days once he located the wreck; but he never located it. A few months later he announced plans to explore the *Florencia*, the flagship of the Spanish Armada supposedly lying sixty feet down in Scotland's Tobermory Bay with a fortune aboard. Once more actual operations never got under way.

In December of 1932 he demonstrated a baby submarine, the *Explorer*, in Long Island Sound. Only twenty-two feet long, the *Explorer* required a mother ship as tender, to which she was connected by two air hoses. Carrying a crew of two and two passengers, she could descend to three hundred feet and crawl forward, backward or sideways. A hatch in the bottom of the hull permitted a diver to leave the vessel for operations on or near the ocean's bottom. In addition, the *Explorer* was equipped with a rake extending from the bow to collect pearl oysters and with a shear-like contraption to clip off sponges. William Beebe of bathysphere fame went down in her and said she seemed to offer interesting possibilities for oceanographic work; others were not so kind—they referred to her as a "milkcan on a matchbox." The following fall Lake announced that he was going to take the *Explorer* on a two-month trip to the Bahamas to locate virgin sponge beds and then on to Venezuela to fish for pearls. And then, he said, the *Explorer* would help him recover the four million in gold and silver bullion aboard the *Lusitania*. But still the liner and her fortune eluded him.

By late 1934 he had developed another salvage craft, the *Laksco*, a tiny submarine compartment at the end of a 115-foot access tube dropped from a surface ship. With this he planned to hunt for the *Hussar*, a British battleship supposedly sunk near New York City's Hell Gate during the American Revolution. Like the *Lusitania*, the *Hussar* was supposed to have a fortune aboard. By the following August Lake had found three hulks, but none of them was the *Hussar* and none had gold. A Miss Mildred Stone ventured down in the salvage craft to look for sunken treasure. *The New York Times* reported the results of her foray: "She came to the surface with one pail, rusty, and one-half of a clamshell in poor condition. Everybody else got grease stains on his clothes." One year later, in September of 1936, Simon Lake proclaimed success at last, but again the hulk was not that of the *Hussar*. He had spent a fortune to find a fortune, yet had recovered little more than "one pail, rusty, and one-half of a clamshell in poor condition."

In 1937 Simon Lake's white-pillared Colonial home in Milford, Connecticut, was sold to satisfy his creditors; it was later turned into a funeral home. Undaunted, Lake moved up the street to a two-family house and set up a three-room workshop in a small factory. In World War II his patents were being used by every one of the warring powers. And the voice of Simon Lake still was heard, urging that submarines be used for the non-destructive purpose of carrying cargo. Only today, many years later, is his dream of cargo submarines about to become a reality. Shortly after V-J Day Simon Lake died, on June 23, 1945, in a Bridgeport hospital. Hailed as the father of the modern submarine, Simon Lake made headlines for the last time.

WILLIAM BEEBE

[1877–   ]

Some people would think my life horrible," said William
Beebe at seventy-nine when he was about to leave New York
for an expedition into the Trinidad jungle. Then he added,
"But to me it's the most wonderful in the world."

Equally famous as a scientist, an explorer and a writer,
Beebe had gone into deep jungles, climbed high mountains, and
descended into the ocean in a two-ton steel ball dangling on
the end of a long cable—the first time man had gone so deep,
observed so much, and returned to tell the world about the
marvels of the sea a half-mile down.

During his boyhood in Brooklyn, where he had been born
on July 29, 1877, to Charles and Henrietta Marie Beebe, his
taste for adventure had been fostered by the tales of Jules
Verne, H. G. Wells and Rudyard Kipling. His first explorations did not take place in faraway lands, but in the school
laboratory, where he spent hour after hour peering through
the microscope. At Columbia University the tall, lanky young
man was an avid student, able to get by with five hours' sleep
a night and concentrate despite any distraction. These two
qualities were to serve him well on later travels.

After a year of postgraduate work at Columbia in 1898,

59

twenty-two-year-old William Beebe became curator of birds at the New York Zoological Park (the Bronx Zoo) and soon was named Director of the Zoological Society's Department of Tropical Research. Now his boyhood dreams of adventure could come true.

After a field trip into the heart of Mexico Beebe wrote *Two Bird-Lovers in Mexico,* the first of more than twenty books about his expeditions, tales of true scientific adventures as vivid today as they were when first published. As one critic said, "He can put the thrills of a dime novel into the march of an army of ants and make an opossum hunt as mysterious as a detective story." Theodore Roosevelt characterized him as one of the few men "who combine love of daring adventure with the power to vividly record the things of strange interest which they have seen."

Ex-Rough Rider, ex-President, Colonel Theodore Roosevelt, explorer, naturalist, writer and robust exponent of the outdoor life, was one of Beebe's early idols. Despite nearly twenty years' difference in age, the two men became close friends. Colonel and Mrs. Roosevelt visited Beebe at the Zoological Society's field-station at Kartabo, British Guiana, where Roosevelt noted that Beebe was no sentimentalist about birds: when one was needed in hand for positive identification, Beebe unhesitatingly shot it. In later life Will Beebe said that "T.R." had taught him the three most important words in a scientist's vocabulary—"I don't know."

After World War I Beebe's monumental four-volume *A Monograph of the Pheasants* began to appear. His hunt for rare species led him to Ceylon, Sikhim, Burma, the Himalayas, Borneo and the Malay Peninsula—a journey of 52,000 miles in seventeen months, and not without danger. Beset by hordes of ants and risking discovery by head-hunting Dyaks, he spent hours lying in the thick grass of the Sarawak jungles to observe the mating dance of the pheasants. In the Malay Peninsula he was charged five times by water buffaloes. And he discovered that his Chinese cook had poisoned five people.

Within a few years Beebe had discovered an even more thrilling form of adventure: exploring the underwater world. Then he burst forth with this enthusiastic command to his readers: "Get a helmet and make all the shallows of the world your own. Start an exploration which has no superior in jungle or mountain . . . provide yourself with tales of sights and adventures which no listener will believe—until he too has gone and seen, and in turn has become an active member of the Society of Wonderers under-sea."

The notion of exploring the depths of the ocean had been in Beebe's mind for many years before he actually went underwater. As a trained naturalist of wide-ranging interests and lively curiosity, he was tantalized by the mystery of what actually happened beneath the ocean's surface. Long before Theodore Roosevelt's death in 1919 the two friends had sketched out plans for an underwater observation chamber. Beebe favored a cylinder, but "T.R." stoutly maintained that a sphere would be the only practical device.

Nevertheless, William Beebe's interest in oceanography never took any concrete, definite direction until 1923, when he led the Zoological Society's expedition aboard the yacht *Noma*. The group sailed to the Galápagos Islands, a lonely archipelago in the Pacific about 600 miles west of Ecuador. There, before the expedition was driven off by lack of water, he observed a host of giant tortoises, giant lizards, and unusual snakes, spiders and fish.

The very day he returned from the Galápagos, he was offered, free of charge, the use of the steam yacht *Arcturus* for an oceanographic expedition. The yacht was fitted out with a boom-walk extending thirty feet out from the side of the ship so that the scientists aboard could observe marine life undisturbed by the ship's passage. In addition, astride the bow was fastened an iron platform, which could be raised or lowered to permit better observation of the waters.

In February, 1925, the *Arcturus* sailed from New York for the Sargasso Sea, an area of the Atlantic abounding in seaweed, northeast of the West Indies. Due to recent severe storms, the Sargasso was in such a disintegrated condition that the expedition moved on to the Pacific and the Galápagos, where the group planned to investigate the great cold Antarctic current known as the Humboldt Current. To their surprise, they could not find the slightest trace of it anywhere around the Galápagos at that time.

William Beebe was far too resourceful to let these two disappointments discourage him. Around the Galápagos there was a multitude of fascinating spectacles to watch, ranging from an erupting volcano that sent a river of lava flowing into the sea to an albatross rookery and such marvels of the deep as a one-ton devilfish and thirty-five-foot whale sharks. For ten days the *Arcturus* hovered above one place in the Pacific so that the scientific adventurers could learn everything possible about that single submerged spot. Using dredges and nets and sounding wire, they worked industriously and obtained an amazing collection of fish, shrimp, lobster and so forth. Beebe found that in this one period of concentrated work they learned more than they would have discovered in several months of scattered effort.

And on this voyage of the *Arcturus* William Beebe found a new way of adventuring—underwater with helmet and hose. Just before sailing from New York he had bought his first copper diving helmet, to be set over the head like an upturned bucket. It had two windows in front and was weighted with four ten-pound pieces of lead. Air was pumped down through an ordinary rubber hose by a small hand pump. Although more advanced diving gear was available, this simple apparatus suited Will Beebe's purposes exactly: to be able to move freely through the water and to see the multi-colored drama of underwater life at first hand.

One morning in April the *Arcturus* was moored near the cliffs of Darwin Bay (the famous Charles Darwin had visited the Galápagos in 1835 aboard the *Beagle*). Dressed only in a bathing suit and rubber sneakers, Beebe, helmet over head, clambered down a metal ladder into the waters for his first dive. Standing on a submerged coral reef, he was almost immediately rewarded by the sight of a twelve-foot shark swimming by.

During the stay at the Galápagos, Beebe descended the ladder or lowered himself by rope for hundreds of helmet dives, taking notes on sheet zinc with a pencil tightly bound to keep the wood and lead from separating. Sometimes he took down a motion picture camera enclosed in a waterproof brass box with a small window in front. There was always so much to see and photograph within the fifty-foot radius of vision—long-spined sea urchins, small ladyfish and wrasse, tiger sharks, a scarlet blenny with splashes of golden brown. Soon, using a powerful harpoon, he learned to spear fish beneath twenty or thirty feet of water—not for sport, but for the aquarium the expedition maintained aboard the *Arcturus*.

Throughout all the helmet dives near the Galápagos Beebe was impressed by the somber, purgatorial aspect of the waters. Haiti, which he visited early in 1927, provided a vivid contrast. Its waters, he said, were as brilliant as its flamboyant natives.

The Haitian expedition tried to keep expenses at a minimum by chartering a four-masted schooner, the *Lieutenant*, pitching tents on deck for living quarters, and using the schooner as a floating laboratory. The group planned to prepare a list of Haitian fish and to study life on a coral reef by diving and taking motion pictures.

Here, with the bottom only three or four fathoms away, Beebe's favorite method of descent was to abandon both the rope and the metal ladder, and to drop directly. "It gives a delightful effect of falling slowly—the realization of a nightmare dream which ends safely," he wrote in his colorful book, *Beneath Tropic Seas*, which he dedicated to his second wife, Elswyth Thane, whom he had married in 1927.

In Haiti the waves were high and the water so filled with powdered lime that Beebe often could not see beyond five feet. Wherever the waters were clearer he watched a fascinating variety of undersea life—the cannibal sargassum fish, silversides, herringlets, sponge crabs and many more. To catch specimens for laboratory study he often carried down a weighted fish pole with a red dynamite cap on the end. An insulated wire ran back to the ship so that the cap could be detonated on Beebe's signal.

In the Galápagos William Beebe had dived to forty feet. In Haiti he reached sixty feet. Still he was not satisfied. Some way must be found to penetrate even deeper, where new and exciting forms of life could be discovered. His thoughts turned again to an underwater observation chamber which he and Theodore Roosevelt had discussed many years before. During 1927 and 1928 he considered, and rejected, various plans for deep-sea cylinders. Newspaper stories about his project brought a flood of propositions, one of them from a young engineer and geologist named Otis Barton. Through

64

Robert Fulton

Edmond Halley

Wilhelm Bauer in his Prussian uniform

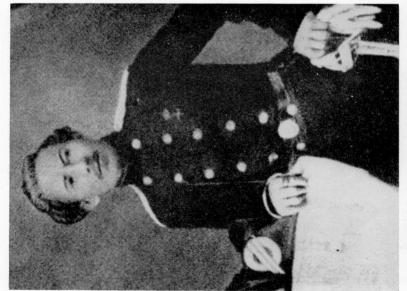

Simon Lake

Auguste and Jacques Piccard aboard the *Trieste*

Rear Admiral Edward Ellsberg at the time of the raising of the *S-5*

Courtesy of William Beebe (Photograph by John Tee-Van)

William Beebe (right) loosening the central wing-bolt on the bathysphere. Otis Barton is at left.

Official U.S. Navy photograph

C. B. Momsen (left) as a Rear Admiral. At right, Rear Admiral D. V. Gallery.

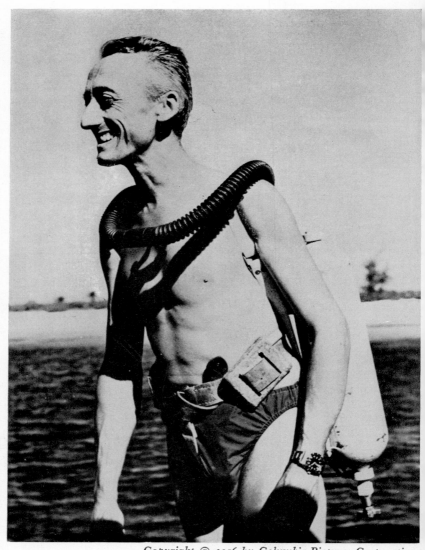

Captain Jacques-Yves Cousteau

Captain Edward L. Beach on the bridge of the *Triton*

Dr. Maurice Ewing. The *Verna* is in the background.

Hannes Keller

a mutual friend, Barton obtained an interview. Beebe soon was convinced that Barton's plans for a steel sphere were workable, and was delighted that Barton would finance the project. The first sphere, constructed with the help of Captain H. J. Butler, was too heavy for the available winches to lift, so Barton had it melted down and recast. At last, by the spring of 1930, everything was ready.

In April William Beebe and his staff—John Tee-Van, Gloria Hollister and Jocelyn Crane—set out for their field laboratory on Nonsuch Island, which the Bermuda government had given them the previous year. Five acres, partly wooded, with alternating coral rock and sandy beaches, Nonsuch was an ideal spot for marine observation: water a mile deep was just a short distance off shore. Soon Otis Barton was on hand with the great steel sphere, which Beebe named the bathysphere.

After several unmanned tests, Beebe and Barton squeezed through the fourteen-inch hatchway into the four-and-a-half-foot interior. For six-foot-one William Beebe it was cramped quarters, with no place to sit except on the cold, hard floor. (Beebe later discovered he had made himself even more uncomfortable by sitting on a monkey wrench throughout the first trial.) A terrific din followed as the crew hammered wrenches to tighten the ten nuts holding the 400-pound door in place. Inside were the oxygen tanks and the trays containing powdered chemicals to absorb moisture and carbon dioxide.

At exactly one o'clock on June 6 the 5,400-pound bathysphere was hoisted by a winch from the deck of the barge. Suspended merely by a single non-twisting steel cable less than an inch in diameter, the great white ball splashed into the water in a froth of foam and bubbles. A second thin cable carried the wires for the light and telephone.

As the two men descended through the vivid blue water that seemed to become bluer every moment, they were fully conscious of the peril in which they had placed themselves, fully conscious that never before had any man gone down so far as they planned to go and returned alive. Peering excitedly out of one of the two eight-inch windows of fused quartz (a third window had proved impracticable, and the extra opening was filled with a steel plug), Beebe phoned back his observations to Gloria Hollister on the deck of the barge. At three hundred feet water began trickling beneath the door. With a sudden sputtering, the light switch short-circuited. Then Beebe jumped as he heard a shrieking rasp—were the walls caving in? No, it was only Barton drawing out a palm-leaf fan to keep the air circulating.

On down they went, past 400, 500, 600 feet. Finally, at 800 feet they paused for five minutes—deep enough for the first trip, they decided—and started back up, ducking unconsciously as the bathysphere broke the surface. Emerging after their hour-long trip, the two bathynauts realized from the strained faces of their colleagues on deck that the tension had been much worse above water than below.

Five days later they went a quarter-mile down, a journey much more productive in scientific observation than their first. They saw a silver hatchet fish and a golden-tailed serpent dragon, jellyfish and flying snails, lantern fish and bronze eels, shrimp and squid. Now that he was down in the very region where so many nets had been hauled, Beebe realized that the bathysphere was to be more valuable than he had ever dared hope: so much could be seen that before could only be guessed at.

Actually, even while the bathysphere experiments were going on, the net hauls continued to be an important part of the expedition's work. Every day in good weather the crew went out on the trawler, letting the nets down more than a mile. By the end of 1931, after three years on Nonsuch, 271 trips had been made and 1,334 nets drawn, yielding amazing deep-sea loot.

Just as exciting as the deep dives in the bathysphere were the contour dives. Starting out in the shallow depths near shore, the barge moved out toward deeper waters, gradually lowering the bathysphere farther and farther down. On one of these contour dives a giant reef suddenly loomed up in front of the bathynauts, and they were drawn up and over it just in time to escape destruction.

In 1932 funds were again available for bathysphere dives. From an unmanned test the bathysphere, now painted dark blue, came back filled with water as a result of a leak in one of the new quartz windows. As the central wingbolt on the door was being loosened, the pressure inside the sphere suddenly caused the bolt to shoot thirty feet across the deck with such force it would have killed anyone in its path.

At last the bathysphere was ready for its first manned dive of the year. It was Thursday, September 22, and for two weeks technicians from NBC Radio had been standing by for the first deep-sea broadcast in history; Beebe was to talk by telephone to the deck, where microphones would pick up his comments. At 1:15 P.M. Beebe and Barton crawled inside and started down. At 1,950 feet, now in the region of eternal darkness, the bathysphere began to pitch so badly that the two occupants thought it had broken loose and was turning over. At 2,200 feet they still were rolling badly. There Beebe— phoning back his observations to the radio audience—saw two six-foot barracuda-like fish, with large eyes and a single line of strong bluish lights down their bodies. These Beebe later named "The Untouchable Bathysphere Fish." By 4:08 P.M. the two underwater broadcasters were safely back on the surface. So—amazingly—was a Bermuda lobster which had been wrapped in cheesecloth and fastened outside the bathysphere. Beebe had thought it would be crushed and that its juices would attract specimens for observation. Instead, the hardy lobster had withstood eight tons of pressure in the deep.

Again in 1934, after being exhibited at the Century of Progress Exposition in Chicago, the bathysphere was back on Nonsuch. Dive Number 32 took place in August. As usual, Beebe was phoning observations back to deck, and Barton was taking movies. Down, down, down they went. When they reached 3,028 feet—a half-mile down—Beebe felt it would be unwise to trust the 3,500-foot cable any farther down. There they lingered, with only the steel walls 1¼ inches to 1½ inches thick protecting them from a total pressure of 7,016 tons. Then, up to the surface they sped, up to the warm sunlight from the icy region of utter blackness. After spending three hours confined in the bathysphere, they found the horizon seemed more distant than ever.

The first flash of animal life, the level of eternal darkness, the discovery and description of a new species of fish—these, said William Beebe in his vivid *Half Mile Down*—were among the most exciting moments of the dives. Equally thrilling was the sudden understanding of some mysterious occurrence, such as when he realized that what he had thought were organisms exploding against the window were really luminous emanations from shrimp. From the standpoint of science, the bathysphere dives were of considerable importance because Beebe was able to *see* so much about which the net hauls had given no hint.

Although the bathysphere was not used after 1934 (the only similar device has been the benthoscope, built by Otis Barton in 1949 for a descent to 4,500 feet in the waters off California), its stature is undiminished as a pioneering effort that pointed the way toward such improved deep-sea vehicles as the bathyscaph and others now being developed. Today the bathysphere has a place of honor in the New York Aquarium.

On Nonsuch Island and aboard the schooner *Zaca*, cruising from the Gulf of California to Gorgona Island, Columbia, William Beebe continued his oceanographic work until the early 1940's. Then he made a number of expeditions into the dense Venezuelan jungle and later worked out of the Zoological Society's field-station in the Arima Valley of Trinidad, spending half the year there and the other half at his New York City home. Although he retired in 1952 as Director of the Department of Tropical Research, this remarkable man, at eighty-four, still was working amid the teeming animal kingdom of the Trinidad rain forest. His life, indeed, has been among "the most wonderful in the world."

AUGUSTE PICCARD

[1884–   ]

JACQUES PICCARD

[1922–   ]

On JANUARY 23, 1960, a huge orange-and-white undersea balloon came to a stop 35,800 feet down in the ocean, at the bottom of the Challenger Deep, a pit at the southern end of a vast furrow in the floor of the Pacific Ocean called the Mariana Trench, two hundred miles southwest of Guam. This underwater dirigible, the bathyscaph *Trieste*, had reached the deepest known spot in the ocean, more than one mile deeper than Mount Everest is high. Here was a record that would never be broken: no one had ever gone so far before, and no one could ever go any farther down. Crowded inside the tiny cabin, which protruded like a bubble beneath the float, were Lieutenant Don Walsh of the United States Navy and six-foot-seven-inch Jacques Piccard, intense, energetic son of the bathyscaph's inventor, the brilliant Swiss engineer and physicist, Auguste Piccard.

For the two Piccards, the *Trieste*'s triumph was not a mere matter of breaking records. It was vindication of their unwavering belief that the bathyscaph, meaning "deep boat," would open to scientific exploration every square mile of the vast surfaces of the earth covered by oceans. Together, these two citizens of small, shoreless Switzerland had raised the funds, supervised the construction, conducted the tests, and faced down an international horde of scoffers to achieve one of the most significant breakthroughs in all history.

One of twin sons born on January 28, 1884, to Hélène and Jules Piccard, head of the chemistry department at Basle University, Auguste had first thought of a "deep boat" more than half a century before the *Trieste*'s descent into the Challenger Deep (and nearly three decades before William Beebe dived in the bathysphere). While a first-year student at the Institute of Technology in Zurich, he became fascinated by an account of a German oceanographic expedition aboard the *Valdivia*. As he read of the difficulties the German scientists had met in trying to trawl for specimens from the surface, he decided that a vehicle was needed to carry man beneath the surface to observe underwater life, deeper than a diver could go, deeper even than a submarine could penetrate. This, he reasoned, should be a free-floating, lighter-than-water balloon, ballasted to descend, unballasted to rise, to which an airtight, pressure-resistant gondola could be attached.

Nearly thirty years elapsed before the tall, lanky, gray-eyed Swiss built his first balloon, and then the one he built was for an ascent into the stratosphere, not for a descent into the ocean. Two interests led him upward into space: his desire to study cosmic rays in mass, and his wish—which he achieved—to open up the stratosphere for airplane travel by creating an airtight cabin. Having received a degree in mechanical engineering from the Zurich Institute in 1907 and then a doctorate in natural science, Auguste had become an avid aeronaut. In 1913, with his twin, Jean, he made a sixteen-hour balloon flight from Zurich over Germany and France to measure the density and temperature within a balloon; in 1915 they served a stint in the Swiss Army's lighter-than-air service. Later, the Swiss Aéro-Club permitted Auguste to make several balloon ascents for scientific purposes. By 1930, when he began to build his stratosphere balloon, he had been professor of physics at the Polytechnic Institute at Brussels for eight years and had been married to Marianne Denis for ten. Jacques Ernest Piccard, the second of their five children and their only son, had been born in Brussels on July 28, 1922.

Funds for the project were supplied by the *Fonds National de la Recherche Scientifique*, Belgium's foundation for scientific research, in honor of which the balloon was christened the *FNRS*. The globe-shaped aluminum gondola, only seven feet across, provided a tight fit for the six-foot-three professor, his assistant, Paul Kipfer, and their equipment. The balloon itself, ninety-eight feet in diameter, was to be filled with lighter-than-air hydrogen and ballasted with lead shot. To be sure the shot would not injure anyone on the ground when dropped from the balloon, Professor Piccard stood at the bottom of a huge chimney at the University of Brussels and had the pellets poured down on him from 165 feet above. Fortunately for the future of underwater exploration, he emerged undamaged.

The *FNRS* was to be launched at Augsburg, Germany, where the balloon had been built, a spot far enough from any seacoast to keep the balloon from accidentally landing in the water. Bad weather delayed the first flight until May 27, 1931. That morning Piccard and his assistant entered the gondola shortly after three o'clock. High winds tossed the balloon wildly, and suddenly, without warning, they were borne aloft. In a half hour they had risen more than nine miles, higher than man had ever gone before. Then, too late, they discovered crucial damage had been caused during the unexpected take-off. The valve to release hydrogen for the descent would not work; they were trapped in the stratosphere. Slowly they drifted toward the Adriatic Sea. Luckily, after sunset the hydrogen cooled, and the balloon gradually descended to safety on the Gurgl glacier near Innsbruck in the Austrian Alps.

A second flight, made in August of the following year, carried Professor Piccard aloft to a record height of 10.7 miles. Although less dramatic than the first flight, this one yielded more important scientific data about cosmic rays. When he returned to Brussels, his students carried him on their shoulders in a triumphant procession through the streets; Madame Piccard made him promise never to soar into the stratosphere again.

He made no promise, however, not to descend into the ocean. One day, at an official reception, King Leopold asked Professor Piccard what new projects he had in mind. On the spur of the moment, Piccard replied that he planned to build a bathyscaph. King Leopold showed so much interest that the professor had no choice but to make good his word.

The *Fonds National de la Recherche Scientifique* granted funds, a laboratory was set up to study high pressures, and by 1940 work on the project was well under way. Then the Germans invaded Belgium. Returning to Switzerland, Professor Piccard spent the occupation years designing precision instruments. Jacques attended the University of Geneva and then the Institut Universitaire de Hautes Études Internationales in Geneva.

At the war's end Auguste Piccard was back at the University of Brussels. Limited funds were still available for the construction of a bathyscaph, but the F.N.R.S. stipulated that supervision of the project be shared with a native Belgian, Max Cosyns, who had accompanied Piccard on his second flight into the stratosphere. As in many cases of shared authority, this arrangement was not entirely satisfactory.

The bathyscaph was named *FNRS-2* to show its direct relation to the stratosphere balloon. Its float contained six upright cylindrical tanks filled with aviation gasoline, which is lighter than water and has a very low rate of compressibility under pressure; additional cylinders contained the ballast and the propellant gasoline. Beneath the float was suspended a tiny, airtight cabin, nearly seven feet in diameter, with walls from four to six inches thick. The cone-shaped windows were made of plexiglass, the narrow end pointing inward.

During the descent water was let in at the bottom of the float, equalizing the pressure inside with that outside. Tons of iron ballast were attached to the float by electromagnets. For the ascent, the electromagnets were cut off, dropping the ballast. These electromagnets were ingeniously rigged so that they could *always* be cut off in case of accident, insuring that the bathyscaph would fall *up*. They could also be cut off by a pre-set time switch, so that the bathyscaph could be sent down on unmanned tests.

At last, in the fall of 1948, the *FNRS-2* was ready for action. With the bathyscaph loaded in her hold, and with Auguste Piccard, Jacques Piccard, and Max Cosyns aboard, the Belgian freighter *Scaldis* set out from Antwerp for Dakar —one of the closest spots to Europe with generally calm seas and depths as great as three-and-three-quarter miles.

In October the *Scaldis* dropped anchor near Boa Vista, one of the Cape Verde Islands. Standing by to render any assistance needed was the *Élie-Monnier* of the French Navy Undersea Research Group, with Commandants Philippe Tailliez and Jacques-Yves Cousteau aboard.

After some accidents and mechanical difficulties of the sort that often plague a pioneer undertaking, the day arrived for the first dive. At three in the afternoon Professor Piccard and Théodore Monod, one of the scientists accompanying the expedition, climbed into the sphere. The twenty-two-foot, fifteen-ton *FNRS-2* was hoisted off the deck and into the water. Then the slow, tedious process of filling the float with gasoline started. Sealed in the cabin, the two underwater observers passed part of the time playing chess. With the last bit of ballast added, the bathyscaph sank to the bottom, fourteen fathoms down. After a few minutes, Professor Piccard jettisoned some ballast and the *FNRS-2* rose again to the surface. Although it was now ten o'clock in the evening, the two bathynauts could not be released until all the gasoline had been pumped out and the bathyscaph loaded back on the freighter. When they emerged at three in the morning, they had been inside twelve hours. Even though the fourteen fathom descent, well within the potential of a diver wearing an Aqua-Lung, was not spectacular, it proved that the principle of the bathyscaph was sound.

On November 3, in the Bay of Santa Clara, an important test was made: sent down on her first unmanned dive, the bathyscaph returned twenty-nine minutes later, having descended to 4,500 feet. Professor Piccard was jubilant. But then trouble developed. The seas grew so rough that the gasoline could not be pumped out, and the bathyscaph had not been constructed to be hoisted aboard the *Scaldis* with the gasoline still in it. Piccard made the heartbreaking decision to dump the gasoline, knowing that this would mean the end of the tests. Further heartbreak lay ahead: the *FNRS-2* still could not be loaded, and the float was badly battered by the tropical squall before safety near the shore could be reached. Jacques Piccard returned to his position as an assistant in economics at the University of Geneva. Sixty-four-year-old Auguste Piccard flew back to Brussels, disheartened but not defeated. Criticized for the mishaps on the tests, the indomitable Swiss never once gave way to doubt.

By 1950 a second bathyscaph was under construction, the *FNRS-3*, using the cabin from the *FNRS-2* with a newly designed float. The *Fonds National de la Recherche Scientifique* had received so much adverse publicity as a result of the unsuccessful 1948 expedition that the project was turned over to the French Navy. Auguste Piccard and Max Cosyns were retained only as "scientific advisors."

Despite misgivings, Auguste Piccard undertook his new role with tremendous enthusiasm. He made several trips to Toulon, where the new bathyscaph was being constructed, but he felt that little progress was being made and that his suggestions were unwelcome to the French. In the meantime, Jacques had gone to Trieste to do research for a thesis in economics; several prominent citizens suggested that the Piccards build a bathyscaph there. Auguste and Jacques Piccard accepted the offer. Considerable sums of money were contributed by individuals and organizations in Switzerland; Italian industry provided manpower and technical and financial aid. Soon the new bathyscaph, the *Trieste*, was being built.

The floats of both new bathyscaphs were designed to be towed with the gasoline in. A shaft ran through each float so that the crew could enter and leave the cabin on the open sea; this shaft would be flooded when underwater to equalize the pressure. The essential difference between the two floats was that the float of the *FNRS-3* resembled the hull of a real ship, whereas that of the *Trieste* was almost cylindrical, and stronger in relation to its weight. Two tanks were provided to take on water to make the float heavier for the plunge. The *Trieste* had propellers beside the float (not beneath, as in the *FNRS-2*), and its cabin was constructed of forged steel, rather than cast, and was therefore much better able to withstand pressure on ultradeep dives.

By August, 1953, the completed *Trieste* had been transported to Castellammare di Stabia, a small port facing Vesuvius in the southern part of the Gulf of Naples. The Swiss and Italian colors were hoisted, and the tests were under way— to twenty-six feet, then to fifty-three, then to 130. The first deep dive was planned for August 26, south of Capri. The Italian naval corvette *Fenice* cleared an area three miles across so that the *Trieste* would not strike anything when she shot up to the surface. Nevertheless, a speedboat bearing a movie starlet insisted on circling round—until doused by the *Fenice*'s hoses. Down the *Trieste* went, to 3,540 feet, plunging four-and-a-half feet into the mud at the bottom. Ballast was jettisoned and, after a moment's hesitation, the *Trieste* rose from the mud and returned safely to the surface, forty-five minutes after she had disappeared from view.

A month later additional dives were made in the deepest part of the Tyrrhenian Sea off Italy, one to 10,300 feet. No one had ever dived so deep before. Again the *Trieste* almost became mired in ooze; funds were so scarce there had been no money to buy an echo finder to warn of the approaching bottom. When the bathyscaph's inventor, his white hair flowing below his ears, wearing his customary Basque beret and double spectacles, was asked whether he had feared for his life, he replied: "Everyone trusts a railway bridge. We, too, trusted in the eternal laws of physics."

In rough seas, getting from the *Trieste* to the longboat, and from the longboat to the ship, proved very hazardous. "For my part," wrote Professor Piccard in *Earth, Sky and Sea*, "I found this crossing from vessel to vessel much more difficult and dangerous than a dive down to 1,732 fathoms in the *Trieste*."

After the 1953 tests, the two Piccards returned to their home in the village of Chexbres, above the Lake of Geneva in Switzerland, where the townspeople presented them with a beautiful blue cedar in recognition of their achievement. Soon after their return, Jacques was married to Marie Claude, who accompanied him to Naples the following fall for a shallow dive—the first woman (and the only one so far) to descend in the bathyscaph.

Meanwhile, the *FNRS-3* had been completed and was making dives. In February, 1954, piloted by Georges Houot and Pierre Henri Willm, the *FNRS-3* descended to a record depth of over 13,250 feet off Dakar. This record would stand unbroken for nearly six years.

The Piccards had by now nearly exhausted the funds available to them. It was an expensive proposition for two private individuals to own and operate a bathyscaph; a dive to five thousand feet, for example, cost a minimum of one thousand dollars. There was no money for dives during 1955, but in late September and October of 1956, Jacques piloted the *Trieste* in a series of dives for Italian oceanographers. On one of these the *Trieste* reached 12,110 feet.

Then, in 1957, at the instigation of Dr. Robert S. Dietz, whom Jacques had met in London in 1955, the U.S. Navy's Office of Naval Research entered the picture. With Jacques

Piccard acting as pilot, twenty-six dives were conducted from July through October in the Tyrrhenian Sea off Naples with American and European oceanographers aboard. As the results were highly satisfactory, the Navy agreed to purchase the *Trieste* for oceanographic research. By mid-1958 she was en route to her new home, the U.S. Navy Electronics Laboratory at San Diego, California. Jacques Piccard accompanied her.

San Diego was an ideal base because of the deep, usually calm waters nearby; in addition, the area had become a vital, energetic center for oceanographers. The *Trieste*'s thirty-six-year-old Swiss pilot was surprised by the abundance of sea life in the Pacific. From December of 1958 through September of 1959 new dives were made off San Diego. Only two problems developed. One was that the electromagnets required a complicated adjustment in current to function with American ballast; therefore iron pellets were imported from Italy. The other was that the Swiss flag, which Jacques suggested be flown with the American colors (as it had been in the tests off Naples), kept mysteriously disappearing. But Jacques Piccard had triumphed over far worse problems; as swiftly as one flag disappeared, he produced another.

Although official approval had not yet been granted, Project Nekton (a name taken from the free-swimming animals of the sea) was foremost in the minds of Jacques Piccard and his fellow-workers: an attempt at an ultradeep dive to the greatest known depth in the ocean, the Challenger Deep.

"Until man placed himself on the bottom of the deepest depression on earth he would not be satisfied," wrote Jacques Piccard in *Seven Miles Down*. "There is a driving force in all of us which cannot stop, if there is one step beyond. . . . It would be the last great geographic conquest."

Various modifications were made in the *Trieste*. The capacity of the float was increased by 6,000 gallons, and a new and stouter sphere was forged at the Krupp works in Germany. Late in the summer of 1959 word came from Washington to go ahead with Project Nekton.

By November the *Trieste* had been reassembled in Guam, and a small group was ready to embark on one of the greatest scientific adventures of all time. Lieutenant Don Walsh was officer-in-charge; Dr. Andreas Rechnitzer, scientist-in-charge; Dr. Robert S. Dietz, project consultant; and, of course, Jacques Piccard was the *Trieste*'s pilot. Preliminary dives were made, one to 4,900 feet, another to 18,150 feet, still another, in the Nero Deep seventy miles from Guam, to 23,000 feet.

The *Trieste*'s big plunge, Dive 65, took place on January 23, 1960, after a 200-mile tow from Guam to the Challenger Deep. At the last moment an order came through designating the two men to make the dive: Jacques Piccard was not one of them. The son of the bathyscaph's inventor, a man who had devoted more than a decade to championing her cause, the only man in the group who had ever piloted the *Trieste*, he quite properly—and very vigorously—protested the injustice. A clause in his contract with the Navy protected his rights, and at 8:23 in the morning he and Lieutenant Walsh climbed down into the sphere, sealed the hatch, and the plunge was under way.

By 9:20 the *Trieste* had gone down 2,400 feet into the region of blackness. "To me," said Jacques Piccard, "she was a living creature with a will to resist the seizing pressure. Above me, in the float, icy water was streaming in as the gasoline contracted, making the craft ever heavier and heavier.

It was as if this icy water were coursing through my own veins."

At 11:44 they reached 29,150 feet, the height of Mount Everest. At 12:06 they heard an explosion. This could mean disaster, but the dials showed nothing wrong. (Later they discovered that an outside window of no real importance had cracked.) They continued down, down, down, until, at 1:06 P.M., their guide rope touched the bottom at the deepest spot in the entire world.

The pressure outside was eight tons per square inch. Looking out into the area illuminated by the *Trieste*'s powerful lights, at the greatest depth in the ocean, they saw a living creature. It was not a monster out of science fiction, but a fish closely resembling a sole, a foot long and six inches wide, with two round eyes atop his head. Soon another living organism appeared, which seemed to be a red shrimp.

After twenty minutes on the bottom, seven miles down, they began their three-and-a-half-hour ascent, shooting up at 4:56 P.M. into the bright sunshine and the steaming tropic heat. Like Sir Edmund Hillary, Jacques Piccard had achieved the peak in his field.

Dive 65 was Jacques Piccard's last journey in the *Trieste*. After receiving the Distinguished Public Service Award from President Eisenhower, he returned to his wife and child at his home in Lausanne, Switzerland, just a few minutes' walk from the house of his father.

Jacques Piccard has not called an end to his underwater adventures. Back in 1954 his father announced plans for a mesoscaph, a "middle-depth boat" designed to operate at 4,000 feet underwater, which, with vertical and horizontal propellers, will be in effect a submarine helicopter. Probably to be ten feet in diameter and to be made of plexiglass for panoramic vision, it will have robot arms to gather fish or plant life. Together, father and son, with the money from the sale of the *Trieste*, now are working to bring this new creation into being. Funds still are short, for the mesoscaph will cost at least $500,000 to build, a staggering sum for two quiet men to amass.

The *Trieste*, crude though she may be, is still an impressive prototype for the deep ships that will explore the ocean in years to come; and whatever these vehicles of the future achieve, it will be due in large part to the genius of Auguste Piccard and to the unswerving dedication of his son Jacques. The Italian Navy once saluted them as "Admirals of the Abyss," and indeed they are.

EDWARD ELLSBERG

[1891–   ]

Rear admiral Edward Ellsberg, the "all-round miracle man in raising wrecks," spent his boyhood in the Colorado Rockies, hundreds of miles from the sea—and yet the sea was to be the background for his many highly dramatic books and the scene of his own thrilling adventures. Actually, the very absence of any good-sized body of water served to stimulate his interest. After going out on the plains to hunt prairie dogs with a .22, he would come home and lose himself in action-filled tales of ships and seafaring men.

The son of Joseph Ellsberg, a Russian-Jewish immigrant, and of Edna Lavine Ellsberg, Edward had been born in New Haven, Connecticut, on November 21, 1891. At the age of one he was taken west to Denver when his father decided to become a dairyman. Joseph Ellsberg was a determined man; some would have called him stubborn. Young Edward soon developed the same trait, which stood him in good stead in later years—in the icy waters off Block Island, in the steaming cauldron of the Red Sea, or on the coast of England just before D-Day—when he faced situations that other men had called impossible. In the Ellsberg vocabulary the word "impossible" did not exist.

The choice of careers brought father and son into conflict. Edward wanted to enroll in the Colorado School of Mines to become a mining engineer (partly because of his intense admiration for the exploits of the school's football team). Joseph Ellsberg insisted that his son become a lawyer. The father won a temporary victory, and Edward entered the University of Colorado for a pre-legal course. During his freshman year, however, Edward Ellsberg received an appointment to the Naval Academy at Annapolis. Here, he felt, was a career that combined his two enthusiasms, engineering and the sea.

One afternoon in the summer of 1910, an eighteen-year-old midshipman still a bit awkward in his sailor whites, he wandered to a hill overlooking the Academy. There stood a stone cross, topped with marble icicles, dedicated to Lieutenant Commander G. W. De Long and those who perished with him on the 1879 *Jeannette* Expedition to the North Pole. Then Ellsberg ambled back to Bancroft Hall and there paused, fascinated, before the tomb of John Paul Jones, father of the United States Navy. Many years later this afternoon's walk was to bear fruit in two of his most absorbing books, *Hell on Ice: The Saga of the "Jeannette"* and *Captain Paul*.

At Annapolis his intelligence, skill and resourcefulness quickly asserted themselves. He won the Seamanship Cup and the Navigation Sextant and, on two separate occasions, the Navy League Medal for essays on naval subjects. When he graduated in 1914, he was the honor man of his class.

After serving briefly aboard the U.S.S. *Texas*, he was detailed to postgraduate work, first at Annapolis and then at the Massachusetts Institute of Technology, where his two-year course in Naval Architecture was interrupted by the outbreak of World War I. Ellsberg was immediately transferred to the New York Navy Yard. There he reconverted seized German liners into troopships, fitted out minesweepers, and then supervised the construction of the battleship *Tennessee*.

In 1919, now a lieutenant, he was ordered back to M.I.T., a welcome assignment for many reasons, one of them being that a student at nearby Wellesley was Lucy Knowlton Buck, whom he married in June. Their only child, Mary Phillips, was born three years later.

As Planning Superintendent at the Boston Navy Yard, his next assignment, he designed a new evaporator to distill fresh water aboard ship, which soon was being widely used. Then, on loan to the Shipping Board, Lieutenant Commander Ellsberg redesigned and corrected deficiencies in the forced draft and ventilation systems of the S.S. *Leviathan*. All these assignments had called for careful planning, ingenuity, and great technical proficiency. All these qualities—plus a tremendous amount of courage—were needed to meet the challenge of his next detail.

On a cold night in September, 1925, the steamship *City of Rome* was moving north toward Boston. Suddenly, about fifteen miles east of Block Island, tragedy struck. The steamship plowed into the submarine *S-51* just forward of her conning tower. In a few moments the *S-51* had plunged beneath the choppy seas, carrying all but three of her crew of thirty-seven to an icy grave on the bottom.

In the face of a public furor the Navy decided that, impossible as the task seemed, the submarine would have to be raised from her resting place 132 feet down. The bodies of the entombed seamen could then be given proper burial and the ship studied to see how such total disaster could be averted in the future. Although it was planned at first to turn the salvage task over to a civilian contractor, Edward Ellsberg stepped forward and insisted that the salvage could—and should—be handled by the Navy.

His superiors, taking his word that he could achieve the feat, designated him Salvage Officer. For his salvage ship he was assigned the 180-foot U.S.S. *Falcon*, fitted with air compressors, extra wrecking pumps, a recompression chamber for divers, and special winches and bits for handling lines. The *S-50*, sister ship to the sunken *S-51*, was to be used as a rehearsal vessel so that the divers could familiarize themselves with the layout before venturing into the wreck in the darkness of the frigid waters. In addition, three tugs and the repair ship *Vestal* were ordered to stand by.

Thirty-three-year-old Lieutenant Commander Ellsberg had carefully worked out his plans: to seal up the inside of the submarine, expel the flood waters from the undamaged compartments, tunnel under to pass lifting chains, and sink and attach pontoons. No one knew better than he how hazardous an undertaking it was; every step of the work would have to be carried out by courageous men working in solitary peril beneath the treacherous sea. Never before in history had such an attempt been successful.

Operations began in mid-October. Bodies of some of the victims were found immediately and brought to the surface amid grim silence. Day by day the weather grew worse, and each day brought new problems. One of the air induction valves was closed only after twenty dives were made, which took five days. A young diver, L'Heureux, down on his first deep-dive, lost his sense of direction and wandered away from the *S-51*. Soon after being brought to the surface he was seized by a terrible case of the "bends," which hospitalized him for eight months and left him a shrunken wreck of a man.

A crippling attack of the "bends" is one of the things a

diver fears most. Under the tremendous pressure at great depths, the nitrogen in the air a diver breathes is forced to dissolve in his blood, instead of being expelled harmlessly as it is under normal circumstances. If the pressure is suddenly decreased, the nitrogen in the blood bubbles, much as ginger ale bubbles when the cap is removed from the bottle. For this reason a diver is brought up by slow stages, with frequent pauses to allow the nitrogen to leave the blood. However, especially with a novice diver, this slow return to the surface is not an absolute guarantee that he will escape the "bends."

Increasingly stormy weather beset the Navy divers battling in the dark depths and, one by one, the men grew so exhausted they were diving by sheer will power alone. Maneuvering the forty-ton steel pontoons amid the heaving waves became more and more difficult. As winter set in the men were able to dive only one day out of three. Finally, Salvage Officer Ellsberg called a halt.

He was not giving up. The need for more experienced divers was dire, so during the winter he sent twenty men—and himself—to a hastily improvised school for deep-sea diving at the New York Navy Yard. He also set about designing one piece of equipment the salvage workers sorely needed: a torch that would cut steel at high speed underwater. After many experiments he devised a torch that worked well on its tests. One hose carried down hydrogen, another oxygen; once ignited, these provided a constant flame, protected from the water by a steady jet of compressed air carried down by a third hose.

When salvage operations resumed on the *S-51* in late April of 1926, Edward Ellsberg was ready to make his first deep-sea dive, to test his torch himself under actual underwater working conditions. First he dressed in three suits of blue woolen underwear, three pairs of wool socks, and wool gloves. With the help of the other divers, he got into the canvas-covered rubber diving suit, then put on rubber mittens, lead shoes weighing thirty pounds each, an eighty-pound lead belt, and a copper breastplate. After he had tested the telephone receivers, so vital for communication with the surface, the weighty helmet with its glass faceplate was placed over his head and given a quarter-turn to make it secure. He checked his air valve and exhaust valve and then, helped over the side to the descending line, began to slide down, deeper and deeper, until he landed on one of the submerged pontoons. For a moment he was so dizzy he thought he might have to signal to be raised, but he finally overcame the faintness.

Now to test the torch! He adjusted the valves and the flame spurted out. Then he released a jet of oxygen under high pressure. Within seconds the torch cut through a two-inch bar of iron. It worked, and worked beautifully.

The salvage crew struggled on—against the sea, against the unwieldy pontoons, against exhaustion. A major problem confronted them when the time came to pass the lifting chains under the S-51 to connect the pontoons on opposite sides. Amidships the submarine was buried nearly six feet deep in hard blue clay, and the only way to get chains beneath was to dig a tunnel with high-pressure hoses. One diver, trapped when the tunnel caved in behind him, calmly washed his way back out of the mud.

Step by step the work moved toward success. The pontoons were placed; the valves of the S-51 remaining open were filled with cement. Then came a setback, all the more heartbreaking because the task was so near completion. On June 22 a bad storm blew up, and some pontoons and the bow of the S-51 began to rise. Lieutenant Commander Ellsberg had no choice but to try to raise the submarine immediately. The premature attempt failed. The valves had to be opened and the pontoons sunk again.

Nearly two more weeks of hard work followed. Then, shortly after two o'clock on the afternoon of July 5, the stern was raised, and an hour later the bow broke the surface. The bodies of eighteen officers and men were still aboard. An extraordinary battle against the sea had been won, and, thanks to the brilliant direction of Edward Ellsberg, not a single member of the salvage crew had been lost in the perilous undertaking.

With the *S-51* safely berthed in the New York Navy Yard after a long, tension-fraught tow from her icy grave, Lieutenant Commander Ellsberg gathered together his possessions. After sixteen years in the Navy, topped by nine months of arduous battle to raise the *S-51*, he put on civilian clothes and returned to civilian life as Chief Engineer for the Tidewater Oil Company. In recognition of his extraordinary feat in raising the *S-51*, he was awarded the Distinguished Service Medal, the first time this honor had ever been conferred in peacetime, and in 1927 he was made a Commander in the Naval Reserve.

The peace of civilian life was interrupted much sooner—and more tragically—than he had anticipated. On a Sunday morning in mid-December, 1927, he picked up the paper and was stunned to see that the *S-4* had been rammed by the Coast Guard Destroyer *Paulding* a few miles out of Provincetown. He immediately rushed to the Brooklyn Navy Yard to volunteer his aid and was raced by Navy ambulance, train, destroyer, Coast Guard cutter and lifeboat to the spot where the *Falcon* stood ready to attempt rescue work. As the lifeboat pitched wildly in the waves, he made a perilous leap to the *Falcon* and sprawled safely on her icy deck.

Six men still were alive in the torpedo room of the *S-4*. The rescuers desperately tried to reach them, but for two days a strong gale prevented any work. By the third day, when calm prevailed, the men had perished.

Edward Ellsberg made a dive to survey the situation. As he moved cautiously atop the hull of the sunken submarine, a sudden swell on the surface wrenched his lifelines, throwing him off balance into the dark waters. Grasping for something to halt his fall, he cut his glove on a jagged projection. Here was an added danger: water could leak into his suit, and air could escape, lowering the pressure inside the suit to the point where what is known as the "squeeze" could occur. With the "squeeze," the pressure of the water literally squeezes the diver to death.

Then he hit bottom, twenty fathoms down, and sank into the soft mud, coming to rest at last on a jagged piece of steel wreckage with his lifelines snagged. One possible way to escape involved another dread danger: "blowing up." A diver "blows up" when excess air pressure causes his suit to balloon, shooting him to the surface so rapidly that he is seized by an acute attack of the "bends." Ellsberg, buried alive in the mud on the bottom, decided to take the risk. He let more air into his suit—and soared to the surface. Back aboard the *Falcon*, out of the freezing water, he gratefully downed a "submarine cocktail"—half boiling-hot coffee and half (in those Prohibition days) grain alcohol—and then was hustled into the recompression chamber to forestall the "bends."

With no rescue possible, the *S-4* operation became a salvage task, following the principles Ellsberg had established with the raising of the *S-51*. Leaving the job to others, he returned home on New Year's Day.

Although Commander Ellsberg had had a story published

in the *Youth's Companion* as far back as 1916, there had been little time since then for creative writing. Now, however, the peerless courage of the Navy divers prompted him to tell their story. The result was *On the Bottom*, published in 1929, a book that immediately took its place as a great modern classic of the sea. This was followed by the novel *Pigboats* and by some superb adventure stories for boys, *Thirty Fathoms Deep*, *Ocean Gold*, *Spanish Ingots* and *Treasure Below*. Then, in 1939, came *Men Under the Sea*. Meanwhile, four years before, he had resigned from Tidewater Oil to become a consulting engineer in private practice and to have more time for his writing.

The morning after the attack on Pearl Harbor, he volunteered for active service. Short, stocky, his jaw as outthrust and determined as ever, fifty-year-old Lieutenant Commander Ellsberg was assigned to the former Italian port of Massawa in Eritrea on the Red Sea, where the retreating Italians had, so they thought, scuttled drydocks and ships so effectively that salvage would be impossible. But in fifty years Edward Ellsberg had never learned the meaning of "impossible."

Arriving in Cairo in March, he learned how crucial his mission was. The previous December six Italian frogmen wearing dark rubber suits, fins, and helmets with a rebreathing apparatus, had infiltrated Alexandria harbor and planted mines under two battleships, the *Valiant* and the *Queen Elizabeth*. These frogmen—who preferred to be known as chariotteers—rode two each astride a cigar-shaped submersible twenty-two feet long, which carried a detachable warhead with an explosive charge. Even though the mines did blow up, the British had captured two of the frogmen in time to learn of the impending explosion and forestall complete destruction. No lives were lost and the ships were kept from sinking. However, the disaster completely tied up the Alexandria drydock, making the restoration of Massawa all the more imperative.

In this summer of 1942, Massawa was, said Edward Ellsberg, "the worst hell hole on earth," a mass of tangled wrecks of every conceivable size, shape and description. At the start he had no salvage ship, practically no equipment, and a civilian crew consisting merely of two salvage supervisors, eight mechanics, and five divers, four of whom he had hired away from Hollywood motion picture studios. For additional workmen he had to draw on the Italian prisoners of war and the natives; he cajoled the British into lending what equipment he needed. And, up in the cool hills, an American civilian contractor, in charge of the payroll for Ellsberg's men, did everything possible to obstruct the work at Massawa, where a valiant little group labored in the blistering heat.

Within a month every sabotaged Italian workshop on the base was working at full capacity, and by May 11 Ellsberg was ready to start raising a giant drydock that would prove of tremendous help to the war effort in the Mediterranean.

This massive drydock, built in the shape of a capital U, had a bottom 100 feet wide, 600 feet long, and fifteen feet deep; its walls were thirty-five feet high and fifteen feet thick. Seven of its eight watertight sections had been damaged by bombs, and in the eighth lay another bomb, still unexploded. And the whole monstrous object was down under fifty feet of steaming Red Sea water.

First, Edward Ellsberg himself went down to inspect the damage. Preparing to dive into the hottest ocean on earth, he donned only cotton underwear under his suit instead of the three pairs of woolens he had worn in the frigid waters off Block Island. This was a mistake: cotton offered little protec-

tion from the chafing of the suit. On all future dives he required his men to wear wool, despite the heat.

After inspecting the drydock, he formulated his plan: to
raise the dock as if it were a diving bell by making the tops
and sides of the walls airtight and then filling them with air,
which would force the water down and out and make the
dock buoyant. Before this could be done, the bomb had to be
removed. Ellsberg and another diver, gingerly juggling the
deadly explosive, managed to get it out and turn it over to a
demolition team. Nine days after work started, the dock was
fully and safely afloat. Soon Massawa was functioning ef-
ficiently as a repair port for damaged British ships.

As a reward for this and other monumental achievements
at Massawa, Ellsberg was speedily promoted to captain. But
the months of battling the sun and the sea had taken their toll:
by November, when Eisenhower invaded Africa, Ellsberg
was wan and shrunken, a shadow of his former self. He and
his men had worked from April through October in Massawa,
a period that—traditionally—was unbearable for white men
even in idleness.

When he received orders to report to Eisenhower's headquarters in Algeria as Principal Salvage Officer for the entire
Torch Area, the assignment seemed a boon, even though he
found harbors full of wrecks from Casablanca in Morocco
through Oran in Algeria to Bône on the border of Tunisia.
There were ships wrecked by American gunfire during the
invasion, ships sabotaged by the resisting French, ships bombed
by the Nazi planes or torpedoed by U-boats. Oran harbor
alone was littered by the wrecks of twenty-seven French and
two British vessels. In addition to salvaging these wrecks,
there was a constant call to repair shattered ships which
miraculously managed to limp into port.

The scorching heat of Massawa was absent here, but Captain Ellsberg again faced shortages of equipment, of trained men, of time. But he still had an apparently limitless supply of courage, resourcefulness, ingenuity and endurance.

And there were many thrilling moments: the frantic attempt to keep the torpedoed H.M.S. *Porcupine* afloat in heaving seas . . . the apparently deliberate sabotage by a French pilot who rammed a sunken cargo vessel loaded with casks of wine, just as Ellsberg and his gallant crew were ready to raise her . . . the valiant but futile struggle to quench the flames devouring the British troopship *Strathallan* . . . the amazing rescue of the anti-aircraft cruiser H.M.S. *Pozarica*, which even her captain had given up for lost.

For nearly a year now, Captain Ellsberg had been pushing himself beyond the limits of human strength. Finally the punishment told. On Lincoln's Birthday he was in the air over the Atlantic, bound for home and a rest.

After two months at the Navy hospital in Bethesda, he was assigned to supervise warcraft building at some thirty shipyards in the New York area. A year of this was enough; eager to return to the war zone, he was assigned to the headquarters of the U.S. Naval Forces in Europe. There, due largely to his intervention, a tragic mistake was averted.

To make sure the Allied invaders would have at least one undamaged port on the French coast, an artificial harbor was to be taken across the Channel on D-Day. Operation Mulberry, as it was called, involved pierheads, gigantic concrete blocks from which breakwaters were to be made, and massive steel arches for floating steel roadways.

Partly submerged for concealment from enemy planes, the massive pieces of this artificial harbor were located at the village of Selsey Bill on the English coast. As soon as he saw what the operation involved, Ellsberg realized it was the equivalent of raising a hundred sunken cargo ships in practically no time at all. And the Royal Engineers in charge of the operation obviously lacked the proper equipment to accomplish the task. Thanks to Ellsberg's persistent objections, changes finally were made. As a result, when D-Day arrived Operation Mulberry was a success: the artificial harbor reached Omaha Beach in good working order.

For his work during the war Edward Ellsberg was awarded the Order of the Commander of the British Empire by Great Britain, two Legions of Merit by the United States, and was promoted to Rear Admiral.

The University of Colorado recognized his important contribution to naval science with a Doctor of Engineering degree, Bowdoin College with a Doctor of Science degree. For his outstanding contribution to the literature of the sea, he has been made a Doctor of Humane Letters by the University of Maine.

Since the war, in his home in Southwest Harbor, Maine, he has continued writing, including those vivid accounts of his war experiences: *Under the Red Sea Sun, No Banners, No Bugles* and *The Far Shore.*

Perhaps the best summation of his career can be found in one of his own books. Although he was writing of the courageous men who had served under him, his words apply equally well to his own life:

"There had been no banners flying, no bugles blowing, nothing at all of the glory of war about the setting, nothing at all but danger. . . ."

C. B. MOMSEN

[1896–   ]

AFTER the submarine *S-4* sank off Provincetown in December, 1927, with a loss of forty lives, Congress—urged by a shocked American public—appropriated money for the Navy to use in developing effective submarine safety devices. One of the young officers detailed to this duty, Lieutenant Charles Bowers Momsen, had an urgent personal interest in preventing further submarine disasters. Just a few months before the *S-4* plunged to her death, six-foot "Swede" Momsen had been in command of her sister ship, the *S-1*.

"Swede" Momsen, who has been said to look and act exactly like an old-time Scandinavian sea captain, is part north German and part Danish, not Swedish. Born in Flushing, New York, on June 21, 1896, to Hart and Susie Bowers Momsen, educated in Washington, D.C., and St. Paul, Minnesota, husky "Swede" Momsen nearly capsized his naval career before it got properly afloat. The trouble arose over a course in Spanish during his second year at the Naval Academy. He disliked Spanish, failed the course, and promptly found himself dismissed.

But "Swede" Momsen was just as tenacious as his square jaw indicated. He persuaded his Minnesota Congressman to reappoint him to Annapolis, and once he was back in, he stayed in. While a midshipman he played football and baseball, and when commissioned an ensign in June, 1919, he was in the top fifteen percent of his class.

After serving aboard the battleships *Oklahoma* and *Maryland*, he reported for submarine training at the New London, Connecticut, Submarine Base in September, 1921. Following a year's service aboard the submarine *O-13* in the Canal Zone, he was given his first command, the *O-15*. Shortly after taking over as skipper, he learned at first hand how swiftly and unexpectedly disaster can strike in the "silent service." Out in the Caribbean the *O-15* suddenly plunged steeply at full speed. Hitting bottom, she buried her bow fifty feet deep in the mud, and there she remained, stuck fast. "Swede" Momsen thought quickly. "Flood the torpedo tubes," he ordered. This done, he then had the water blasted out. The desperate tactic worked, and the *O-15* floated free.

After commanding the *R-24* and *S-1*, he served tours of duty with the Bureau of Construction and Repair and with the Submarine Safety Test Unit. It was during this period that he helped develop the now-famous submarine escape device known as the "Momsen Lung."

Several decades earlier Robert H. Davis of Siebe, Gorman, Ltd., the world's largest diving equipment firm, had invented the Davis Submerged Escape Apparatus. However, in the late Twenties, when Lieutenant Momsen began work on the "Lung," the D.S.E.A. was regarded as impractical by the United States Navy. Momsen and his associates started from scratch. Carefully, systematically, they tested one method after another, conducting experiments that called for a tremendous amount of courage. No previous records existed to indicate what the outcome might be. At their disposal the

Navy had placed a reconditioned submarine, fitted out as a floating laboratory—none other than the salvaged *S-4*, a vivid and constant reminder of the significance of their task.

Finally Momsen felt he had a device to test in an actual escape from the depths. On February 5, 1929, a Navy ship was anchored at Smith Shoals, eleven miles off Key West, Florida. Tension ran high as the officers and men looked out across the water. For there, forty feet down, the *S-4* was submerged, with Lieutenant Momsen and Chief Torpedo Man Edward Kalinowski aboard, preparing to venture an escape wearing the "Lung."

Down in the *S-4* Momsen and Kalinowski worked swiftly to fasten the "Lungs" to their bodies by straps and clamps. The "Lung," resembling a cross between a hot-water bottle and a gas mask, consisted of a breathing bag with a capacity equal to that of the human lungs. One tube carried air from the mouth to the bag; another tube, enclosing a container of soda lime to purify the air of noxious carbon dioxide, carried air from the bag to the mouth. With the "Lungs" securely fixed, the two men filled them with oxygen from a large flask, adjusted the mouth-pieces, and fastened nose clips in place.

Meanwhile, they had flooded the compartment so that the entrance to the escape hatch was covered and the pressure within the compartment equaled the water pressure outside. Now they opened the hatch and shoved out a buoy to which an ascending line was attached, knotted every ten feet to indicate the stages where they should pause briefly to allow for decompression.

Aboard the Navy ship there was a great breath of relief when the buoy bobbed up on the surface. So far, everything was going well. A few moments later the two heroic experimenters broke through the waves. They were so elated by their success in escaping from the conning tower that they returned to the *S-4* to make another escape, this time from the motor room. Again everything worked according to their calculations, and they moved up the ascending line to the surface without difficulty. Although there was no need for it on the test, the inflated "Lung" would have provided enough buoyancy to keep them afloat for a considerable time.

One test followed another, each one deeper than the one before. On March 6 Momsen and Kalinowski escaped from 160 feet down, and on March 7 from 204 feet. When, shortly after, twenty-six men wearing "Lungs" managed a test escape near New London, the "Momsen Lung" had proved itself beyond a doubt. For having "courageously, repeatedly and voluntarily risked his life in conducting experiments," Lieutenant Charles Bowers Momsen was awarded the Distinguished Service Medal. Chief Gunner Clarence Tibbals and Frank Hobson, a civilian engineer of the Bureau of Construction and Repair, who had worked with Momsen in devising the "Lung," were also honored. In an editorial praising this remarkable achievement, *The New York Times* pointed out that the "Momsen Lung" was the only one of 4,971 designs submitted to the Navy board that had even been worth attention.

It is Navy custom for officers to receive varied training, and in the early 1930's one of Lieutenant Momsen's assignments was unusually varied: technical director for several Hollywood pictures about the Navy starring such unlikely seafarers as Tallulah Bankhead and Jimmie Durante.

September, 1932, saw "Swede" Momsen on duty at the Submarine Base at Pearl Harbor. Then, after service on the minelayer *Oglala* and on the submarine *Canopus* and the

Augusta, he was called back from the sea in August, 1937, to become officer in charge of experimental diving at the Navy Yard in Washington, D.C. This was the sort of opportunity Lieutenant Commander Momsen always welcomed.

Two surgeons from the Navy Medical Corps were detailed to work with him to find a substitute for nitrogen to dilute the oxygen used by divers. After countless tests they discovered that helium had definite advantages. Divers absorbed less than half as much helium as nitrogen, and helium showed much less tendency to dissolve in the body fats, thus diminishing the danger of the "bends." But the greatest advantage to the use of helium was the reduction of narcosis, usually associated with nitrogen, and for this reason divers could go deeper.

With painstaking care Momsen (who by now had become a qualified diver himself) worked out a new set of decompression tables for divers coming up from dives of varying depths and different lengths of time. Using the new helium-oxygen mixture and the new decompression tables, divers could now descend 200 feet beyond the former safety level of 300 feet. The only drawback was that helium, which conducts heat better than nitrogen, conducted the diver's body warmth right out into the cold water, leaving the diver shivering. To remedy this, the diver was provided with electrically heated underwear.

The Navy had now gone twelve years without a single submarine disaster. On the morning of May 23, 1939, that record was tragically broken. Eight miles out of Portsmouth, near the Isle of Shoals, the *Squalus* plunged on a routine test dive. Suddenly, because an engine induction valve failed to close, the engine room flooded—flooded so quickly that twenty-six members of the crew had no time even to grab for the "Lungs" with which, by now, all submarines were equipped.

Thirty-three officers and men were still alive, battling to stop the descent. Their efforts were futile. The *Squalus* settled to the bottom, 243 feet down. As the submarine was below the safety limit set for the use of the "Lung," her skipper, Lieutenant Oliver Naquin, decided to wait in the hope that he and his men might be saved by the rescue bell which had been developed some years before by Momsen and Commander Allan McCann, who had relieved him in the Bureau of Construction and Repair.

Luck now was with the *Squalus* survivors. The stricken submarine was quickly located, and the following morning the salvage ship *Falcon* was on hand with Lieutenant Commander (soon to be Commander) Momsen and his divers aboard. Carefully the ten-ton rescue bell was lowered over the side and guided into position over the escape hatch, where it was fastened much as if it were a vacuum cup. Once the water was blown out of the lower compartment of the bell, the two men operating it could open a hatch into this compartment, and from this compartment open the hatch of the *Squalus*. Swiftly Lieutenant Naquin designated six seamen and an officer for the first trip. After they had crawled up into the bell, the two hatches were closed, the vacuum broken, and the bell started its trip to the surface.

By the time darkness fell, two more trips had been made and all but nine of the survivors rescued. Then the fourth and last trip started. Suddenly, just 150 feet from the surface and safety, the lines tangled. Everyone aboard the *Falcon* worked feverishly. After four seemingly interminable hours the bell and its occupants finally were hauled on deck. Never before in underwater history had so many men been rescued from such a depth.

As usual, Lieutenant Commander Momsen was loathe to treat his feats as a matter of heroics. He was quoted as telling reporters at the scene that it was "nothing more than a practical application of drill work that had been taught at the Navy's submarine schools for eight years."

The task of salvaging the *Squalus* still remained. Under Momsen's direction, the divers made 640 dives in the next few months, under the most severe conditions, to bring the stricken submarine to the surface. Modest, soft-spoken "Swede" Momsen was commended by the Secretary of the Navy for his "high and outstanding measure of ability, exceptional coolness, judgment, specialized knowledge and responsibility." To his superiors—and to the men whose lives he saved—his work was no mere "practical application of drill work."

In September of 1939 he assumed command of the *Sirius* and two years later was detached for duty at Pearl Harbor, where he remained until early in 1943. From February of that year until June, 1944, Captain Momsen served as commander of two submarine squadrons, where his valor and courage again brought him distinction.

The United States submarine campaign against the Japanese was being imperiled by faulty torpedo exploders which caused an alarming number of "duds" during attacks on the enemy. "Swede" Momsen personally took over the investigation to find out what was wrong. During the tests one torpedo fired into a cliff failed to explode. Unhesitatingly, Momsen stripped off his uniform, dived in, swam down to where the torpedo lay in nearly twenty feet of water, examined it, and then assisted in its recovery for further analysis. As a result of his careful and patient investigation, a vastly improved exploder was developed in which he coordinated his own ideas with those of others. The effectiveness of American submarine attacks increased tremendously.

During this same period he commanded the first U.S. submarine "wolf pack." A master of submarine warfare, he organized submarines into an attack group capable of operating deep in the Japanese-controlled East China Sea at full striking power. Submarines under his command sank many thousands of tons of Japanese shipping.

After duty in Washington with the Office of the Chief of Naval Operations, he commanded the battleship *U.S.S. South Dakota* for seven months, participating in pre-invasion operations against Japan, including attacking enemy installations in the Tokyo area. The story is told that, during his command of the *Dakota,* an explosion suddenly occurred below while Vice Admiral W. A. Lee was aboard. Momsen calmly ordered the magazines flooded. When Admiral Lee asked whether everything was under control, Momsen replied, "We'll know in thirty seconds. If the magazines aren't flooded, the ship will blow up."

Following a brief detail with the Navy Department in Washington, Rear Admiral Momsen was named administrator of the U.S. Naval Shipping Control Authority for the Japanese Merchant Marine, where he directed the repatriation of nearly six million people from China, Manchuria, Formosa and the Pacific islands. This complex operation included training unskilled Japanese crews and then integrating United States and Japanese shipping into an effective organization.

After further duty in the Pacific and Washington, Momsen served for three years as Assistant Chief of Naval Operations for Undersea Warfare, a newly created post with wide responsibilities for both submarine and—increasingly important —anti-submarine developments. Then he spent two years as Commander Submarine Force, Pacific Fleet, followed by duty as Commandant of the First Naval District in Boston. While stationed there he married Mrs. Anne I. Schmidt of St. Petersburg, Florida, the second marriage for both. By his first marriage he has a daughter and a son, also a naval officer.

"Swede" Momsen's last tour of duty was as Commander Joint Task Force Seven. On September 1, 1955, he was transferred to the retired list. Among his many decorations are the Navy Cross, the Distinguished Service Medal from both the Army and the Navy, and the Legion of Merit with two Gold Stars and Combat "V." On his retirement he was advanced, on the basis of combat awards, to the rank of Vice Admiral.

In more than twenty years of use the "Momsen Lung" performed valiantly. Since 1952 submarine escapes have been accomplished by such methods as "free ascent" and "buoyant ascent," and recently the "Steinke Hood" (an apparatus consisting of an inflatable life jacket which feeds air to a hood worn by the diver) was used by its inventor in an escape from a simulated depth of 450 feet at the Navy Experimental Diving Unit in Washington.

But all during the perilous days of World War II it was the "Momsen Lung" that served the "silent service." No one knows how many men it helped to escape from shattered submarines, just as no one knows how many American lives were saved as a result of "Swede" Momsen's determination to discover the reason for "dud" torpedoes. One fact is clear: C. B. Momsen is one of this country's foremost underwater heroes.

MAURICE EWING

[1906–   ]

O<small>N A</small> rocky cliff high above the west bank of the Hudson River, a beautiful estate spreads out to cover a hundred wooded acres, complete with palatial residence, garage, greenhouse, and swimming pool. Here lives a tall, broad-shouldered, tousle-haired Texan, Maurice Ewing.

He also works here, for this magnificent spot near Sneden's Landing, New York, is the site of Columbia University's Lamont Geological Observatory. Maurice Ewing has been its director since its establishment in 1949. Once the home of financier Thomas W. Lamont, the big stone residence now houses one of the world's best-equipped laboratories for geophysical, geochemical and biological programs. The garage is a storehouse for sea-bottom samples. The greenhouse has become an instrument shop, and the swimming pool is used for laboratory work. An old root cellar contains a battery of seismographs, sensitive instruments designed to detect and plot earth tremors within a few moments. And down on the river is the anchorage for the three-masted *Vema*, a 202-foot, 553-ton schooner, the sea-going laboratory on which Maurice Ewing and his associates have conducted some of the most fascinating work being done today in the science of oceanography. Although primarily a geophysicist, Dr. Ewing has devoted most of his attention to oceanography since three-fourths of the Earth's surface lies beneath water.

A tireless worker and passionate scientist, Maurice Ewing has described himself as "a big, rough-looking character." Six-foot-two, with piercing blue eyes and shaggy gray-brown hair, he has a preference for old clothes and no fear of getting his heavy, capable hands dirty with work.

He developed his capacity for hard work early in life. One of seven children of Floyd and Hope Hamilton Ewing, William Maurice Ewing was born on May 12, 1906, in Lockney, a small farming center in northwest Texas. To earn his way through Rice Institute in Houston, he worked as a library assistant during the winters, and in the summers he served with the crews of various oil companies prospecting off the shores of Texas and Louisiana. The crews dumped explosives into the water and recorded the times the echoes came back in order to determine whether the sound had possibly traveled through oil beneath the water. Young Ewing's curiosity was aroused by the fact that sound waves moved at different speeds through the same water; he later discovered that the various layers of the ocean bottom conduct sound at different velocities.

While he was a junior at Rice, his first article appeared in *Science*, "Dewbows by Moonlight," in which he described walking around the campus at two o'clock in the morning to measure the angles of the moonlight's reflection from the dew on the grass. Graduating with honors in mathematics and physics in 1926, he received an M.A. degree the following year and also became a fellow in physics. Rice awarded him his Ph.D. in 1931.

After a year teaching physics at the University of Pittsburgh, he joined the staff of Lehigh University in 1930, remaining on the faculty until 1944. In the nearby Pennsylvania cement district, he continued his experiments with shock waves by taking measurements when blasting was being done in the quarries. During the summer of 1934 the twenty-eight-year-old Texan and two other scientists spent their vacation tossing blasting gelatin from a whaleboat into the sea a hundred miles off the Virginia coast. The shock waves set up by the underwater explosions were recorded by a seismograph trailing from a nearby vessel of the United States Coast and Geodetic Survey. The data gathered this summer yielded valuable information about the nature and extent of the continental shelf stretching out from North America into the Atlantic.

As a Guggenheim Fellow, and then as a research associate at the famous Woods Hole Oceanographic Institution in Massachusetts, Ewing continued his seismic measurements of the ocean basins. Woods Hole, like the Scripps Institution of Oceanography at La Jolla, California, was (and is) a world-famous center for the training of oceanographers. In 1941, Columbus O'Donnell Iselin, director of Woods Hole, collaborated with Maurice Ewing and J. Lamar Worzel on a pioneer manual for underwater sound transmission. Ewing and Worzel also made improvements in the means of measuring gravity from submerged submarines, and with A. C. Vine they developed the bathythermograph, a device for measuring the temperature of water at various depths.

Soon after the United States entered World War II, Dr. Ewing wrote to the Department of the Navy suggesting that underwater sound transmission might be used to locate ships in distress or planes downed at sea. The survivors would explode small depth charges, the vibrations from which could be picked up by listening posts many miles away. The source of the vibrations could be figured quickly by mathematics, and the ship or plane in distress located. The proposal was rejected. The vibrations, said the Navy consultants, would not travel far enough to be of any use.

Then a young Navy lieutenant, E. L. Newhouse III, convinced that the idea would work, persuaded his superiors to give it a trial. In April, 1944, Maurice Ewing was aboard a yawl anchored off the Bahamas. Dangling at the end of 4,000 feet of cable reeled out from the craft was a hydrophone, an instrument resembling a stethoscope with electrical amplifications. A hundred miles away a Navy destroyer escort, dropping four-pound depth charges at hundred-mile intervals, moved off to a distance of 1,200 miles. On the yawl, working with earphones and a recorder, Maurice Ewing was able to hear clearly all the explosions, even the one farthest away.

Naval officials, tremendously impressed, called the discovery SOFAR (Sound Fixing and Ranging), and authorized Dr. Ewing to perfect it. By late 1945 he had succeeded in transmitting sound underwater from Dakar on the West African coast to Bermuda; the vibrations traveled more than 3,000 miles in sixty-two minutes. For this work, which has been called the most important discovery in communications since radar, Ewing received the Distinguished Public Service Award in 1955, the Navy's highest civilian honor.

Simultaneously with his work on underwater sound transmission, Maurice Ewing had been exploring the deep in another way—through underwater photography. He had begun his pioneer experiments in 1938 while cruising aboard the Woods Hole research vessel *Atlantis*. The first camera, enclosed in a pressure-resistant aluminum case, was designed to take a series of pictures on striking bottom. The ballast to make it sink was attached by a block of salt; when the salt dissolved, the ballast was dropped and the camera returned to the surface. When this device was lost on its third trial, a second camera, enclosed in a Pyrex glass test tube five feet long and six inchs wide, was designed to take two pictures on each trip underwater. This too was lost when it collapsed under pressure at 1,500 fathoms.

A third instrument, with a trigger to set off a clockwork mechanism controlling the exposures when the camera hit bottom, was successful. By late 1944 Dr. Ewing reported that this camera had taken successful black-and-white photographs more than three miles down, a remarkable feat never before achieved.

In 1947, now a Professor of Geology at Columbia University, he set out with an expedition aboard the *Atlantis* sponsored by the National Geographic Society, Woods Hole and Columbia. The group intended to survey the previously unexplored Mid-Atlantic Ridge, the world's longest mountain range, a chain extending underwater almost the whole length of the Atlantic.

A number of fascinating methods were employed to discover information about the origin, age and history of the ridge. TNT was set afloat with toy balloons for hourly explosions throughout the entire trip; by this means the depth of the water and the sediment beneath were measured and the peaks and valleys of the ridge were charted. To gather specimens of the fantastic deep-sea fish living in the waters around the Mid-Atlantic Ridge, the scientists drew trawls—thirty-foot mesh bags, held open by steel frames.

Samples of sediment were collected from the bottom by a method known as "coring." Basically, sea-bottom sediment is cored just as an apple is cored, only the oceanographers use a vastly larger instrument. Steel tubes up to seventy or more feet long, two-and-a-half inches in diameter, with a sharp cutting edge, are dropped down, heavily weighted, at the end of two to three miles of steel wire. The tube cuts into the sediment and brings back cores which, when dried and studied, reveal valuable information about the area where they were collected.

Here, too, Maurice Ewing continued his experiments with deep-sea photography, lowering on a wire a pole to which a camera and flashlight had been attached. When the pole hit bottom, a trigger opened the shutter and set off the flash; and at the same time a miniature coring tube at the end of the pole took a sample of the spot that had been photographed. During the second of these Mid-Atlantic Ridge expeditions, he took color photographs at depths of 900 to 2,400 feet, the first time in history color pictures had been taken at depths greater than 600 feet.

Year after year he continued his oceanographic cruises, tracing the Hudson River Canyon into the Atlantic a hundred miles farther than anyone had known it existed, discovering a mile-high, mile-deep underwater mountain off the Massachusetts coast and a vast new underwater canyon in the western Atlantic.

To help Dr. Ewing and his associates at the Lamont Geological Observatory in their work, Columbia University acquired its own research vessel, the *Vema*. By 1961 the *Vema* had made seventeen scientific voyages, some of them lasting nearly a year, at the cost of more than $1,000 for each day.

Aboard the *Vema* Maurice Ewing had a close call with disaster. Just after dawn on a January morning in 1954, the schooner was suddenly caught by a ferocious gale 200 miles north of Bermuda. Dr. Ewing, his brother John, also a scientist at Lamont, and two officers rushed on deck to lash

down precious equipment. Without warning, two mountain-
ous waves crashed down on the ship, sweeping the four men
overboard into the heaving seas. Not one of them had a life-
jacket.

As he struggled to tear off the clothes dragging him under,
Ewing could hear the cries of the drowning first mate. Gradually the sounds grew weaker and then ceased altogether. In
the distance he could see the *Vema* heave to—to pick up his
brother, he later discovered. Battered by the waves, he tried
swimming, then floating, growing more and more exhausted
moment by moment. Then a voice shouted nearby; it was
the second mate, clinging to an oil drum. Dr. Ewing grabbed
the other end. After forty minutes in the seething waters the
two were finally sighted and rescued.

Time and time again aboard the *Vema* Maurice Ewing and
his associates have conducted intriguing investigations. Ewing
had pioneered the adaptation for magnetic surveys at sea of an
airborne magnetometer used during World War II for submarine detection; this device has been used continuously on
all of the *Vema*'s cruises. Ewing and his associates took seismic
observations from the bottom of the Gulf of Mexico that
turned out to be identical with observations from the mid-
Atlantic, thus disproving the theory that the floor of the Gulf
had once been above water. Another theory they disproved
was that the Grand Banks fishing grounds off Newfoundland
were geologically a part of the Atlantic. In 1961 they made
the first recording of an earthquake by a seismograph dropped
to the floor of an ocean—near their field station at St. David's,
Bermuda—thus opening up striking new possibilities for underwater research.

With geologist-meteorologist William Donn, Maurice
Ewing has advanced a startling new Ice Age theory. Briefly,

this theory suggests that a sudden warming of the Atlantic Ocean melted the Arctic Ocean's ice sheet. Water evaporating from this ice sheet condensed and fell as snow on the northern parts of the continents, forming glaciers which gradually grew so large they cut off the Arctic Ocean from the warmer Atlantic. The Arctic again froze over, and the glaciers, no longer nourished by snow, gradually melted. However, the temperature of the Arctic now seems to be rising again, and if the ice cover disappears, gigantic glaciers may again start forming.

Honor after honor has been conferred upon Dr. Ewing: the American Geophysical Union's William Bowie Medal, a Doctor of Science degree from Lehigh University, the Argentine Navy's Order of Naval Merit. In 1960 he became the first winner of the newly established Vetlesen Prize in Geophysics—consisting of a gold medal and $25,000—in its field the equivalent of a Nobel Prize.

With his second wife and their four children, Maurice Ewing lives in a house on the very edge of the Lamont grounds, overlooking the Hudson River on its way to the sea. He has said he would just as gladly have tackled the moon, rather than the ocean, had the opportunity for original research there been offered him first—and he is now developing a seismograph to operate on the moon. Fortunately for our knowledge of oceanography, this towering Texan scientist went to sea, instead of into space.

JACQUES-YVES COUSTEAU

[1910–   ]

FEW MEN have done more to spur others on to the exploration of the underwater world than Captain Jacques-Yves Cousteau. As co-inventor of the Aqua-Lung, he has enabled thousands to swim with the freedom of fish to discover the wonders that lie at hidden depths. His book, *The Silent World*, has been read by millions, and the motion picture of the same name has been seen by audiences all over the world. From his remarkable research ship, the *Calypso*, he has hunted for wrecks and archaeological remains, searched for oil, and made the deepest anchorage ever achieved by man. "Next to General de Gaulle," it has been said, "he is the best-known Frenchman in America."

On June 11, 1910, this intrepid undersea adventurer was born to Daniel P. and Elizabeth Duranthon Cousteau at their country home in Saint-André-de-Cubzac, a village near Bordeaux, France. His father was a widely-traveled lawyer, and when Jacques-Yves was ten the family spent a year in New York, living in an apartment on upper Broadway. During the summer Jacques-Yves and his brother Pierre went to camp in Vermont. As a boy he showed considerable technical flair, and by thirteen he had begun making his own home movies.

In fact, his hobbies took so much of his time that his father had to threaten stern discipline to get him to concentrate on his studies at the Stanislas Academy in Paris, from which he graduated in 1927.

The sea drew him on, and he entered the Naval Academy at Brest. After graduating, he enrolled in the fleet's air school. Then, just as he was about to finish the course, a catastrophe occurred—but not in the sky, or on the sea. Late one night, when he was driving his father's sports car, the vehicle swerved wildly out of control, crashed, and rolled over several times. Although Jacques-Yves escaped alive, one arm was broken in several places and the other was paralyzed. As the broken arm mended he worked tenaciously to regain the use of the other. Flying was permanently out of the question, but if he could get the arm to function, there remained a career with the sea, of which he had explored only a small portion of the surface.

After months of struggle, he conquered the paralysis. Stationed at the Toulon Naval Base in the mid-Thirties, the long-legged, blue-eyed midshipman took to swimming in the Mediterranean to strengthen both arms. At Toulon he met a slightly older naval officer, Philippe Tailliez. At night the two would take turns in the wardroom shooting arrows from a submarine gun, using an old piano as a target. During the day, whenever off-duty, they practised diving with watertight goggles and rubber foot-fins. Undersea hunting, popularized by Guy Gilpatric in his ever-delightful book *The Compleat Goggler*, was then the reigning sport along the Riviera, and Cousteau and Tailliez pursued it avidly. Soon they met a civilian diver, Frédéric Dumas, who hunted underwater with a rubber slingshot and curtain rods for arrows. The three companions were soon to win fame as the first of the "men-fish."

Exciting as goggle-hunting was, Cousteau found that he could not penetrate deep enough into the water or stay down as long as he wished. He began to experiment to find some device that would enable him to breathe underwater without being restricted by the traditional diver's air hose to the surface. First he tried an apparatus invented a few years before by Yves Le Prieur, a French naval officer. A single cylinder of compressed air was worn on the chest; the diver operated a valve to regulate the flow of air to his mouth. Because this device could be used only for short dives, Cousteau persuaded a gunsmith aboard ship to help him build an oxygen rebreathing outfit of his own design, in which soda lime purified the oxygen passing from the cannister back to the diver's mouth. Testing this apparatus at forty-five feet down, he was seized with terrible convulsions. He improved the design and tested his new device; again convulsions nearly cost him his life. The trouble, he discovered, was that oxygen was toxic at the depths he wished to reach.

When the outbreak of World War II scattered the team, Cousteau, now nearing thirty, served as gunnery officer aboard the cruiser *Dupleix*. After the fall of France, the three skin divers found themselves again in Toulon, where they made their first underwater motion picture, the eighteen-minute *Sixty Feet Down*. Then, in November of 1942, the Germans moved into southern France, and the French fleet was scuttled.

Cousteau, with his official naval duties at a minimum, became a fearless worker in the French underground, accomplishing missions which later won him the Legion of Honor. He also continued his experiments with a self-contained underwater breathing apparatus to allow the diver to swim on nearly equal terms with the shark and the manta. Late in 1942 he went to Paris, where he met Émile Gagnan, an engineer with the Air Liquide Company, who had devised an automatic regulator for feeding cooking gas to automobiles. It would work just as well, they decided, feeding compressed air to a diver.

Early in 1943 Cousteau prepared to test his first Aqua-Lung in the Marne just outside Paris. It consisted of three cylinders of compressed air, a regulator about the size of an alarm clock, and two tubes, one for intake and the other for exhaust, joining in a mouthpiece. The regulator insured that the diver would receive the proper amount of air to keep his lungs at the same pressure as the water pressing upon them. On the first test the Aqua-Lung worked perfectly when Cousteau swam in a horizontal position, but not when he stood up or bent down. Soon Cousteau and Gagnan figured out that the regulator had been placed too high, a fault easily corrected.

Cousteau and his companions tested the device in a sheltered cove on the Riviera. As Cousteau went under, it was an anxious moment. On the shore Dumas waited tensely, ready to dive at the least sign of trouble. Cousteau's wife, Simone, swam along the surface, breathing through a snorkel tube, looking down to observe every movement of her tall, lean husband. Below, Cousteau soon felt a surge of triumph: the Aqua-Lung worked flawlessly.

Cousteau and blonde Simone Melchior, descendant of an old French naval family, had been married in 1937. This summer of 1943 they lived in a small villa with their two sons, Jean-Michel, four, and Philippe, two. Also crowded in the villa were Dumas, Tailliez and his wife and child, and several others. For food—scarce during the Occupation—they relied mainly upon a store of black beans. Yet all summer long the three menfish worked unceasingly, diving with the Aqua-Lung day after day, curious to discover as much as they could of this unexplored underwater world. They devised an underwater motion picture camera and, because motion picture film was unavailable, spliced together rolls of film intended for miniature cameras. With these makeshift devices they made their second motion picture, *Sunken Ships*, in which they recorded their fascinating explorations of the wrecks in the Toulon and Marseilles area.

As they gained experience, they ventured deeper and deeper, always watchful of the physiological effects. In October Dumas reached a depth of 210 feet. There he was seized by a strange sort of drunkenness, which has since been called nitrogen narcosis, or "rapture of the deep." It is probably caused by oversaturation with nitrogen, and although it disappears immediately when the diver swims to a shallower depth, it is extremely dangerous. While the diver is overcome with the "rapture," he loses his judgment and may even be deluded into discarding his mouthpiece, with fatal consequences.

When the German Occupation ended, Cousteau, by dint of persuasive arguments, managed to obtain permission from the naval authorities for the experimental work to continue. They were, at first, given a rather indefinite schedule calling for mine-sweeping, salvage, and the training of divers. This was the beginning of the G.E.R.S., *Groupe d'Etudes et de Recherches Sous-marines*, the Undersea Research Group. Tailliez later wrote that the "creative will power" of Cousteau was largely responsible for the success of the Group.

Using themselves as guinea pigs, Cousteau, Tailliez and Dumas made tests of the effects of underwater explosions on divers, discovering that a near-naked diver fares better than one wearing a suit and helmet. They removed two torpedoes from a scuttled German battleship and assisted in the removal of many mines. Then the government decided to test the Aqua-Lung as an escape device for men trapped in a submarine. During the course of these tests Cousteau and his companions made the first motion picture of a submarine moving underwater, *Une Plongée du "Rubis."* In addition to showing men escaping from a submarine, the film portrayed the firing of torpedoes and the laying of mines.

Probably the most dangerous moment in Cousteau's career occurred in August, 1946, when he and other members of the Group sought the answer to the mystery of the Fountain of Vaucluse, near Avignon in France. Although the Fountain is calm for most of the year, for five weeks in March a bubbling jet suddenly shoots up from the siphon and floods the River Sorgue.

Linked to each other by a thirty-foot safety rope, much as mountain climbers are linked, Cousteau and Dumas began their descent down a rope into the water of the siphon. Cousteau was wearing his newly perfected constant-pressure diving suit, which affords insulation against cold and protection against pressure. Slightly under 200 feet down they struck a sloping beach, still underwater. Each noticed the other was floundering around in a strange manner. Bewildered by the maze in which they found themselves, they could not find the hole leading from the elbow of the siphon, where they were, up the other arm of the siphon to an inner cavern. They seemed to be suffering from a strange sort of nitrogen narcosis, for they were depressed rather than elated. For a moment Dumas lost his mouthpiece; before he could replace it he swallowed a great deal of water. In desperation, dragging Dumas, Cousteau began to ascend, finally remembering to give the six tugs on the rope signalling that they should be pulled up. When they reached the surface, they were deathly pale and nauseated.

Later in the afternoon Tailliez and another member of the Group ventured into the siphon, only to be overcome by the same strange heavy intoxication. The following day a laboratory analysis of the air in their cylinders showed that, because their new compressor had taken in its own exhaust fumes, each cylinder had contained a dose of carbon monoxide lethal at the depths to which they had descended.

The following summer Cousteau and the Group made further tests to see how deep divers wearing the Aqua-Lung could go with safety. Cousteau, Tailliez and Dumas all managed to sign their names on a board nearly 300 feet down; they were, however, so dangerously overcome by "rapture" that they realized this was far below the safety limit. At about 260 feet, on the return journey, the "rapture" suddenly vanished.

That fall their experiments had a tragic outcome. Maurice Fargues, one of the Group, managed to write his name on a board 396 feet down. But there, seized by "rapture," he abandoned his mouthpiece. When he was brought to the surface his comrades worked twelve hours trying to revive him —in vain. In 1948 Dumas, quite unintentionally, broke the existing record for a free-diver breathing compressed air. Surveying a wreck, he became so fascinated he lost track of how deep he was going. Climbing aboard ship later, he learned that he had penetrated to 306 feet and returned safely.

By now the Undersea Research Group had acquired an ocean-going tender, which they christened the *Élie-Monnier*. With this ship they were at last equipped to undertake more extensive, and more serious, oceanographic work, which had been Cousteau's ambition from the start. Early in the summer of 1948 they searched in the bay outside Tunis for traces of one of the harbors of ancient Carthage. Then they began investigating an ancient galley sunk about 80 B.C. off the coast of Tunisia, near Mahdia. After five days of arduous and often frustrating work, they located the galley at a depth of 130 feet and later raised four huge, barnacle-encrusted pillars and two gigantic anchors. This pioneer work opened up an immense field of research to submarine archaeologists.

Later that year the *Élie-Monnier*, commanded by Cousteau, set out from Toulon for Dakar and the Cape Verde Islands, to assist in the first trials of Professor Piccard's bathyscaph. After a number of unfortunate and unforeseen accidents, the trials came to an abrupt end when a strong gale forced them to dump the expensive gasoline ballast and battering waves badly damaged the float. Cousteau, however, had the wisdom to see how remarkable the Piccard invention was, and he was instrumental in persuading the French Navy to undertake the building of the second bathyscaph, the *FNRS-3*, which later made several record-breaking descents into the depths. Cousteau went down in the *FNRS-3* as an observer on a descent into a 5,300-foot underwater canyon off Toulon when the underwater dirigible started an avalanche. Cousteau and the pilot, Georges Houot, found themselves and their craft buried in the mud nearly a mile down. As neither man was one to panic, they carefully figured out how much ballast should be dropped, and soon they were on their way to the surface.

In 1950 Jacques-Yves Cousteau took leave from the French Navy to undertake oceanographic expeditions aboard his own research vessel, the *Calypso*, a reconditioned 360-ton, 141-foot-long former British minesweeper built in the United States. It is a remarkably well-equipped ship for the scientific study of the sea, and it has grown more remarkable each year, with the addition of dredges, coring devices, powerful winches, a submerged underwater observation chamber in the bow, a well by which divers can go direct from the ship into the sea, a diving platform, and, of course, special equipment for the making of Captain Cousteau's amazing motion pictures of the silent world. Outstanding among its gear are the Submarine Scooters devised by Captain Cousteau—yellow electric torpedoes which will carry a diver through the water at three miles per hour.

Captain Cousteau took the *Calypso* on her first oceanographic expedition, to the Red Sea, where he made the first color photographs ever to be taken 150 feet down in the twilight zone. Rigid color controls were used so that the true values of the spectrum would be obtained.

Starting in mid-1952 he directed a monumental archaeological undertaking, raising from the bottom of the Mediterranean, off Marseille, the ruins of a Greco-Roman cargo ship. To leave the *Calypso* free for other work, a base was established for the divers on a windswept cliff on the Grand Congloué, the island near which the wreck is located. The vessel, probably the oldest cargo ship ever discovered, is supposed to have foundered about 230 B.C. Using compressed-air suction pumps to clear away the mud and shoot the ship's treasures up to the surface, the divers have recovered more than 8,000 amphoras, earthenware jars used to store such cargo as cereal, wine and oil. Underwater television was used successfully to direct part of the work.

Cousteau sailed the *Calypso* to the Persian Gulf in 1954, and there Aqua-Lung divers probed the ocean bed in search of oil for the Anglo-Iranian Oil Company. Then he sailed on to the Indian Ocean, to take soundings off the islands of Aldabra and Comoros. The following year, on a long voyage through the Mediterranean, the Red Sea, the Indian Ocean, and the Persian Gulf, he made films for the motion picture *The Silent World*, which won the Grand Prize at the Cannes International Festival and an Academy Award. Among those accompanying him on this voyage was James Dugan, one of the first Americans to recognize Cousteau's unique genius, and the author of a fascinating biography of Captain Cousteau, *Undersea Explorer*, as well as the entertaining history of undersea exploration, *Man Under the Sea*.

On returning to the eastern Mediterranean, Cousteau and Dr. Harold Edgerton of the Massachusetts Institute of Technology tested a new deep-sea camera the latter had developed. The camera, weighing 100 pounds and constructed to withstand pressure up to 17,000 pounds per square inch, was lowered on a nylon cable to 14,000 feet. The photographs they obtained were the first ever taken at that depth in the Mediterranean.

The *Calypso* then set out to explore the Gulf of Guinea. Aboard, as on many other trips, were Madame Cousteau and young Philippe Cousteau, as well as a full complement of scientists. Off the Ivory Coast of Africa, the vessel paused over a deep furrow in the Atlantic's floor known as the Romanche Trench. There the anchor was dropped on a special nylon cable five-and-a-half miles long. The anchor held, 25,000 feet down. It was the deepest anchorage ever achieved by man.

On this same trip the *Calypso* oceanographers experimented with a new automatic electronic flash camera developed by Harold Edgerton. Enclosed in a steel tube capable of withstanding pressure up to eight-and-a-half tons per square inch, the camera was designed to begin taking four pictures every minute after having been down two hours. The camera was lowered to 24,600 feet and left down for three hours. After it had been brought up and the film developed, the experimenters were jubilant. Even though only two pictures had been obtained, those two were very clear, and they had been taken a half-mile deeper than any photographs ever before.

In recent years the *Calypso* has continued doing important work in undersea geology, biology and hydrology. Now she carries aboard her a revolutionary new underwater vehicle developed by Captain Cousteau—a jet-propelled diving saucer, built to survey the continental shelf at depths beyond the reach of divers. Slightly over six-and-a-half feet in diameter and five feet thick, the diving saucer has a steel, pressure-resistant hull, around which are wrapped the motor, jet pump and batteries, enclosed in Fiberglas covers. Completely rudderless, she is steered up, down, or sideways by maneuvering her jet nozzles. A hydraulic claw will be added to pick up specimens from the bottom.

Now in his fifties, still so lean he seems taller than his five-feet-eleven-inches, silver-haired Captain Cousteau heads a multitude of projects with the energy, patience and intelligence that have distinguished his remarkable career. Most of the profits from his Aqua-Lung patents and from his film company, Associated Sharks, go toward supporting the *Calypso* expeditions and his other oceanographic projects. In 1952 he founded the now-flourishing French Undersea Research Center at Marseilles and, upon retiring from the French Navy with the rank of *capitaine de corvette* in 1956, he became director of Monaco's Oceanographic Museum, founded by the pioneer oceanographer, Prince Albert I, great-grandfather of Prince Rainier. In 1959 he was elected president of the World Underwater Federation.

One of his most recent projects is a *biatron*, a sort of concrete apartment house for fish, where sea animals can be herded and bred underwater much as cattle and pigs are on land. A three-mile area of the seafront in Monaco has been set aside for this pioneer work in underwater agriculture. Other projects include newer and better vehicles in which man can peacefully invade the sea. The "creative will power" that sparked the French Navy's Undersea Research Group several decades ago is still very much in evidence.

EDWARD L. BEACH

[1918–   ]

O NE DAY in 1916 the cruiser *Memphis* of the United States Navy was riding quietly at anchor off Santo Domingo, where American marines had just been landed to occupy the Dominican Republic. She was commanded by Captain Edward L. Beach, author of such popular books for boys as *Robert Drake at Annapolis*, *Dan Quin of the Navy*, *Ensign Ralph Osborn* and *Roger Paulding, Apprentice Seaman*. All at once a gigantic tidal wave engulfed the ship, dashing her against the rocks, with a loss of thirty-three lives. Although Captain Beach gallantly shouldered full responsibility, an investigation by the Navy cleared him of any blame, and he went on to other commands, including that of the battleship *New York* during World War I.

Two years after the *Memphis* disaster, on April 20, 1918, in New York City, Captain Beach and his wife, Alice Fouché Beach, became the parents of a son, Edward L. Beach, Jr. He was to become the second Captain Edward L. Beach, career officer, popular author, and skipper of the nuclear-powered submarine *Triton* on her historic circumnavigation of the globe.

After graduating from high school in Palo Alto, California,

Edward L. Beach, Jr., entered the Naval Academy at Annapolis in 1935. An active athlete and bright student, he was selected as the midshipman who had done the most to promote naval spirit and loyalty in his regiment. He was also, according to stories told later, a young man inclined to take his responsibilities very seriously. One story has it that when Orson Welles made his famous 1938 radio broadcast about an invasion from Mars (a broadcast so realistic that people panicked all across the nation), Ned Beach, then commanding the regiment of midshipmen, turned out his men and reported to the commandant that they were ready to repel the Martian invaders. (His version is that he was the only one who actually turned out.)

Graduating second in his class, he was commissioned an ensign in June, 1939, and assigned to duty aboard the cruiser U.S.S. *Chester*, but in September, with the outbreak of war in Europe, he was detailed to the U.S.S. *Lea*, an old "four piper" destroyer which cruised up and down across the North Atlantic on Neutrality Patrol. During his two years' duty on the *Lea* he became so attached to the old ship that, when orders arrived in September, 1941, transferring him to Submarine School, he requested permission to remain with the *Lea*.

But the Bureau of Navigation was short of applicants for submarine training, and Ensign Beach—as ordered—reported to the school at New London, Connecticut. Once there, he set to work with determination. In December—just after the devastation of Pearl Harbor—he graduated with the highest standing in his class. By now he had been instilled with the spirit of the submariner: an unshakable loyalty to his ship, a vital trust in his shipmates, and a passionate respect for the sea.

On New Year's Day, 1942, he reported to the U.S.S. *Trigger*, then being fitted out at the Mare Island Navy Yard in San Francisco. After months of intensive training and trial runs, the *Trigger* and her crew departed for the war zone in May, stopped one day at Pearl Harbor, and then sped off to meet the Japanese fleet massing to attack Midway. Just short of her goal the *Trigger* ran aground on a submerged coral reef. By the time she had pulled herself off, the Battle of Midway was over. This was the only time in her valiant career that the *Trigger* failed to appear where the danger was greatest.

By spring of 1943 the *Trigger* had completed five patrols, exploring the waters of the Pacific from the Aleutians to the Equator, sinking freighters and tankers and destroyers. She managed to damage a brand-new Japanese aircraft carrier so badly just as the carrier poked her nose out of Tokyo harbor that rumors flew about that the vessel had been hit as she slid off the launching ways. She had crept close to the coast of Japan to plant a mine field and, hundreds of feet beneath the surface, she had shuddered under the shattering impact of enemy depth charges. Her crew had known the elation of seeing their torpedoes explode on target, and they had known the frustrating despair of firing other torpedoes that turned out to be faulty or "duds." Time after time, month after month, the *Trigger* and other submarines had trouble with "dud" torpedoes until, at last, an official investigation was made and the flaws corrected.

Lieutenant Beach, having served as assistant engineering officer and engineering officer, was now executive officer. When the *Trigger* returned to Pearl Harbor in June for extensive repairs, he was flown back to the United States for three weeks' leave. He visited his father, seventy-six and seriously ill, for what he knew would be the last time. And, in Palo Alto, he met Ingrid Bergstrom Schenck, the blue-eyed daughter of a Professor of Geology at Stanford University. One year later she was to become his wife.

In the fall Ned Beach was back at Pearl Harbor, and the *Trigger* was ready to depart. On her next four patrols she again covered herself with glory. She sank nineteen ships and damaged four others. She survived encirclement by an entire Japanese convoy, and she managed to send to the bottom the ComJapSubPac—the commander of Japanese submarines in the Pacific. In May, 1944, new orders arrived for Lieutenant Beach, which he read with regret. He was detached from the *Trigger*—his home and his mistress for two-and-a-half years—and ordered to Portsmouth, New Hampshire, for duty with the submarine U.S.S. *Tirante* when commissioned.

In a service that boasted many outstanding officers and men, Ned Beach had distinguished himself; hard-working, thorough, idealistic, he combined an unbeatable spirit with absolute determination. When he reported to Portsmouth he wore his new lieutenant-commander stripes, and he had with him his bride of less than a month.

The *Tirante* set out for Pearl Harbor in the early days of 1945, and from there she moved on to her first war patrol in the East China and Yellow Seas. For this, her maiden effort, the *Tirante* received the Presidential Unit Citation, her commanding officer received the Congressional Medal of Honor, and her executive officer, Lieutenant Commander Beach, received the Navy Cross. Ned Beach accepted his honor with a heavy heart. In late March, while still on patrol, the *Tirante* had been ordered to rendezvous with his old ship, the *Trigger*. But the *Trigger* did not appear—then or ever again. For her, as for so many others, the record read "Overdue, presumed lost."

June of 1945 saw Lieutenant Commander Beach with his own command, the submarine U.S.S. *Piper*. The *Piper* penetrated mine fields barricading the Straits of Tsushima, between Korea and Japan, to carry out operations in the previously inaccessible Sea of Japan. News of peace brought an abrupt halt to her mission. Her skipper had a double reason for rejoicing: he had just learned of the birth of a daughter.

After six-and-a-half years' service at sea, twenty-seven-year-old Lieutenant Commander Beach returned to the United States to become aide to the Chief of Naval Personnel and then to serve in the Atomic Defense Section of the Chief of Naval Operations.

While there he met another naval officer, a tough, caustic genius, Captain Hyman G. Rickover, who was fighting to persuade the Navy that an atomic submarine was both a possibility and a military necessity. He had drafted a letter for the signature of Admiral Nimitz, then Chief of Naval Operations, stating that the atomic submarine was "militarily desirable."

Quickly perceiving the immense importance of Rickover's project, Lieutenant Commander Beach did everything he could to assist, carrying the draft letter about with him and marshalling convincing arguments as to why it was imperative for the Navy to start work on an atomic-powered submarine. By the end of 1947 the letter had been signed, and the first steps were being taken to make the *Nautilus* a reality.

Shortly after, Ned Beach was back on sea duty, as commanding officer of the submarine U.S.S. *Amberjack*. During war games Beach and the *Amberjack* made themselves the bane of many an admiral aboard an aircraft carrier. For one thing, the *Amberjack* maneuvered so skillfully she never could be located. And then, to make matters more exasperating, a photograph of the carrier would arrive, taken through *Amberjack's* periscope, with a message scrawled at the bottom, "Regards from *Amberjack*." The carriers might not be able to find the *Amberjack*, but she certainly could find them!

Beach's next assignment, in September, 1949, was to the newly created post of Naval Aide and Assistant to the Chairman of the Joint Chiefs of Staff, General Omar Bradley. Less than two years later, Commander Beach was once again headed toward the sea—as skipper of the new *Trigger*, during her construction and first commissioning. It was while he was commanding the second *Trigger* that his first book appeared —*Submarine!*—a moving, rousing, superbly-written salute to the lost *Trigger* and to the other heroic submarines and submariners of the war in the Pacific.

In 1953 Ned Beach reported to Washington, D.C., for duty as Naval Aide to President Eisenhower, where his reputation for being a "strictly business" officer increased. While he was serving as Eisenhower's aide, the launching of the *Nautilus* approached. A number of operating submariners and officers at the Naval Academy proposed Commander Beach as the first commanding officer of the *Nautilus*. Beach, however, supported the choice of Commander Eugene P. Wilkinson, and it was Wilkinson who, on January 17, 1955, signaled that the *Nautilus* was "under way on nuclear power."

By early 1957 Ned Beach, now a captain and the author of a second best-seller, the novel *Run Silent, Run Deep*, was again eager to be back at sea. He assumed command of the U.S.S. *Salamonie*, a veteran Atlantic Fleet oiler in the Mediterranean. Returning to the United States in December, she distinguished herself—in the midst of a raging North Atlantic hurricane—by an emergency refueling of three destroyers and by rescuing a man swept overboard from one of them.

Captain Beach was then assigned duty with Rear Admiral Rickover for an intensive course of study in submarine nuclear propulsion. This course—already almost legendary because of Rickover's unwavering insistence that the men taking it display unusual iniative, thoroughness, and an absolute determination to succeed—included training in the actual operation of the land prototypes of submarine nuclear power plants. In the fall of 1958 Captain Beach assumed duties as prospective commanding officer of the atom-powered *Triton*, then being constructed at the Electric Boat Division of the General Dynamics Corporation. Because the skipper of a submarine usually is a commander, not a captain, this assignment aroused considerable speculation that something special was in store for Ned Beach and the *Triton*.

Launched in August, 1958, the 447½-foot-long *Triton*, comparable in size to a light cruiser, was commissioned on November 10, 1959—the largest and most powerful submarine ever built. Intended as a high surface speed submarine capable of supplying radar information to a task force, she has two atomic reactors and two entirely independent nuclear propulsion plants of an advanced type, each driving one of her huge twin screws. When Ned Beach received the orders for the *Triton*'s "shakedown" cruise, he was both elated and perplexed—elated because the *Triton* was to make an epochal underwater cruise all the way around the world, perplexed because his men could be given no hint that they would be completely out of touch with their families for nearly three months. His first thought (as he admitted later in an article in *The Saturday Evening Post*) was, "What shall I tell Ingrid?"

The *Triton* was to follow approximately the route charted by Ferdinand Magellan's expedition of 1519–1521, the first to circle the globe. In addition to giving her machinery and 175-man crew a workout, the *Triton* was to carry a half dozen civilian scientists to conduct hydrographic, oceanographic, magnetic and gravitational surveys, amassing valuable data recorded continuously around the world. This, of course, was the primary purpose of the trip.

On February 16, 1960, Captain Beach said good-bye to his wife and three children, and the *Triton* sailed from Groton, Connecticut, to a spot off Montauk Point, Long Island. There she submerged and headed—underwater—toward St. Paul Rocks, a group of small, rocky islands off Brazil about fifty-five miles north of the Equator, the spot to which the *Triton* would return as the reference point of her circumnavigation.

Leaving St. Paul Rocks and planning to round Cape Horn in about nine days, she was forced to change course off the Falkland Islands to rendezvous with the cruiser U.S.S. *Macon*. Her chief radarman was critically ill, and Ned Beach decided that this one man's life was more important than completing the voyage on schedule. At two o'clock in the morning of March 5, the *Triton* broached surface with only five feet of her conning tower out of the water, and, amid rough seas, the ill radarman was successfully transferred to the waiting cruiser. Two thousand miles and several extra days had been added to the voyage, but the ship had not actually surfaced.

Rounding Cape Horn, the *Triton* headed for Easter Island and Hawaii, setting a number of bottles afloat so that the course of currents could later be determined. On March 27,

nearing Guam, she fired her torpedo tubes three times in salute as she passed close to the spot where the first U.S.S. *Triton* is now known to have been destroyed by Japanese depth charges during World War II.

Leaving Guam, Captain Beach proceeded to the Philippine Islands, passing near the spot where Magellan was killed. When the periscope was raised in Magellan Bay, it was face to face with a startled native fisherman. The *Triton* then moved south into the Indian Ocean. Where the Lombak Straits enter the Indian Ocean, there is a swirling change in the water density. When the *Triton* hit this, it was as if a plane had hit an air pocket, and, suddenly, in forty seconds, she made an involuntary dive of 125 feet.

As the submarine moved across the Indian Ocean, a ban on smoking was imposed on the crew, one of numerous tests —both physical and psychological—to which they were subjected. The results of these tests have provided information of widespread value—even for space pilots.

Rounding the Cape of Good Hope on Easter Sunday, the *Triton* returned to St. Paul Rocks on April 25, her historic round-the-world trip completed. Still submerged, she sailed to a point off Cadiz to pay homage to Magellan, who had sailed from there more than four centuries earlier flying the flag of Charles V of Spain. Then she returned to the United States, having covered nearly 42,000 miles in eighty-four days—all of them underwater.

When the *Triton* surfaced on May 10 off Rehoboth, Delaware, a helicopter was waiting to fly her clean-cut, graying skipper to Washington, where President Eisenhower awarded him the Legion of Merit. Four hours later Captain Beach was back on board the *Triton*. Nothing was going to deprive him of the honor of bringing his ship into port after *that* cruise! The next day he was reunited with his wife and children in their home in Mystic, Connecticut, returned from an underwater adventure such as Robert Fulton, Wilhelm Bauer, and even Simon Lake never dreamed of.

There is a postscript to the story. When the *Triton* returned to Groton, observers noted that, instead of a new set of colors, a tattered flag bearing only forty-eight stars flew high above the ship, from the top of her raised periscope. Forty-two-year-old Captain Edward L. Beach explained: it was the flag which had flown over the *Memphis*, commanded forty-four years before by another Captain Beach, on the day when the sea had overwhelmed her.

HANNES KELLER

[1934–   ]

Even though the *Trieste* has reached the deepest known spot in the ocean and Captain Cousteau's diving saucer now is exploring the middle depths, the underwater world still presents man with a stirring challenge: how deep can he go unprotected by armor?

In 1948, wearing an Aqua-Lung supplying compressed air, Frédéric Dumas reached 306 feet—despite the fact that compressed air exposes the diver to the grave danger of "rapture of the deep" below 200 feet. That same year Petty Officer Wilfred Bollard of the Royal Navy, using an oxygen-helium mixture, reached the bottom of Scotland's Loch Fyne, 540 feet down; and in late 1956 diver George Wookey of the Royal Navy descended to 600 feet. But Bollard's decompression took almost seven hours; Wookey's almost twelve. Any free diver seeking to reach great depths must therefore find some mixture of gases that does not cause "rapture" and does not require an extremely long period of decompression to avoid the "bends." A young Swiss mathematician, Hannes Keller, seems to have solved both problems.

Hannes Keller was born on September 20, 1934, in Winterthur, a Swiss town not far from Zurich, the son of architect

Friedrich Keller and Emma Keller-Schneider. The youngest of four children (he has an older brother and two older sisters), he first showed a yen for adventure when he was four years old and wandered merrily away from home, tagging along behind a military band. As he grew older, he was fascinated by outdoor life: he learned to swim and drive a motorcycle and, after only one hour's instruction, to pilot an airplane. His third hour in the air nearly brought disaster: the plane developed motor trouble and a crash seemed imminent. But he refused to give way to panic. "I tried to start the motor again by turning the propeller with the wind at high speed," he says. "Though the plane got over the maximum speed limit approaching the ground, I succeeded and got safely back to the base." He did have some less hazardous pastimes, such as playing the piano, his choice ranging from Chopin and Bach to Bartok and Gershwin.

After finishing his studies at the Winterthur *gymnasium* in 1953, Keller entered the University of Zurich, intending to study philosophy. Soon, however, he switched to mathematics and physics. He was not, he says, an especially good student. Intrigued by the unknown, he wanted to explore and experiment on his own, rather than simply learn facts from books.

His studies were interrupted by the military service required of all young men in Switzerland. One night, while on guard duty at headquarters, a friend began telling him about the excitement and thrills of skin diving. This was a sport Hannes Keller had to try for himself.

His first opportunity came on the island of Elba, between Corsica and Italy. There he dived with a mask only, and the marvels of the underwater world were every bit as wonderful as his friend had indicated. Eager to explore farther—and deeper—he spent six months in Greece diving with a self-contained underwater breathing apparatus he had made himself.

Once out of the service, he completed his work at the University of Zurich and began teaching mathematics at the Technikum Winterthur, a school for engineers in his native village. The challenge of deep-diving still intrigued him, and he started to work out a theory whereby a diver could go deeper than two hundred feet without danger. A mixture containing nitrogen exposed the diver to rapture; a mixture of helium and oxygen required a long and dangerous decompression. It occurred to him that breathing a varying mixture of different gases at different levels during the descent and ascent might overcome the problems.

By late 1959 Hannes Keller was ready to make the first tentative test of his theories. His equipment was homemade. For the equivalent of a dollar he purchased an old gasoline drum. To this he strapped four big compressed-air tanks. With this contraption—and an automobile inner tube for emergency ascent, if necessary—he plunged into the icy waters of the Lake of Zurich. As he descended deeper and deeper into the dark, strange waters, he had some moments of uneasiness over the peril involved. Yet there was no physical discomfort, nor was there any feeling of "rapture"—even at 400 feet. Returning to the surface more rapidly than the standard decompression tables would indicate was possible, he suffered not the slightest twinge from the "bends."

Early in 1960 he took his theories to Dr. Albert Buhlmann of the cardio-pulmonary section of the University of Zurich. Together, he and Dr. Buhlmann sought an explanation of the so-called nitrogen narcosis and translated his theories about gases into a practical working formula. This required working out a complicated new calculation of the relationships between the depth and duration of dives, the varying mixtures of gases to be used, and the speed at which the various gases dissolved in the different parts of the human body.

The computation of these figures would have taken an experienced—and industrious—mathematician a minimum of two years. However, the Zurich Service Bureau of the International Business Machines World Trade Corporation heard of Keller's project. Eager, as always, to assist in scientific developments, IBM offered the use of the IBM 650 computer without charge. In just over four hours the computer checked and calculated more than 250,000 four-figure numbers to compile four hundred new decompression tables, covering depths down to 1,312 feet.

On August 21, 1960, Hannes Keller prepared to descend into the still, clear waters of Lake Maggiore in southern Switzerland. For an hour or two before going down he breathed oxygen to cleanse as much nitrogen as possible from his body. Then, with tanks containing the various gases strapped to his back and clad only in a rubber suit with goggles and mouthpiece, he began the descent. In about four minutes he had reached a depth of 510 feet, and in thirty minutes more he was back on the diving raft, grinning triumphantly. A long-standing concept—that decompression after such a depth required from five to seven hours—had been shattered.

The French Navy's Undersea Research Group at Toulon became interested in his work and invited him to make a further test under their supervision. In Toulon that fall, with Captain Cousteau as one of the interested spectators, Hannes Keller entered the high-pressure chamber. The hatch was closed, and in ten minutes the pressure was raised to simulate that at a diving depth of 820 feet. Forty-nine minutes later he emerged, healthy and happy, to be congratulated by his friends and by the diving experts who had witnessed his feat.

But still he was not satisfied. He was sure his technique could produce even better results than on the 820-foot dive. Night after night, instead of sleeping, he stayed up calculating and computing figures, and at last he devised a formula for a new dive: to descend to 1,000 feet in ten minutes, spend two minutes between 700 and 1,000 feet, and then decompress within thirty-one minutes. His friend Fleury Niggli tells how, at eleven o'clock one night, Hannes, a wide grin almost covering his face, knocked at the door to tell him the news—that he was ready for a dive that would really amaze the experts. "Can't you imagine the puzzled faces of the people who try to understand how it is done—and decide it's impossible!" exclaimed Hannes. "This will be tremendous fun for us, and I'm absolutely sure it will work."

In the spring of 1961 Hannes Keller and his friends again visited the Toulon Naval Base. After one day of preparation, he made the 1,000-foot dive in the high-pressure chamber exactly as planned. The next day he spent ten minutes doing very hard work at a simulated depth of 700 feet. Diving experts from many countries were there to watch the demonstrations, and afterwards one of them remarked, "Only God and Hannes know how this can be done!"

Two weeks later the young Swiss scientist-adventurer came to the United States for his second demonstration to be held at the U.S. Navy Experimental Diving Unit in Washington. There, in the test tank, at a simulated depth of 700 feet, he spent ten minutes lifting a 66-pound weight ten times a minute to a height of two feet. Commander N. E. Nickerson, officer in charge of the E.D.U., commented that he had never before seen a diver work so hard at a greater depth than 200 feet.

Despite these demonstrations before qualified observers, there were still some skeptics who suggested that Keller's technique worked only because Keller himself might be physiologically unique, a "miracle-diver." Even when a thorough examination by U.S. Navy physicians failed to reveal anything extraordinary about his physiology, these detractors still were not silenced: no one but Keller has used this technique, they kept saying.

Someone other than Keller did use this revolutionary technique: *Life* editor Kenneth MacLeish. In June, 1961, he and Keller made ready for a hazardous dive: their goal was a depth of 700 feet in Lake Maggiore, nearly 200 feet deeper than Hannes had gone in his dive the previous summer. Because MacLeish had only three days in which to prepare for the dive, Hannes was to handle the manipulation of the breathing apparatus for both MacLeish and himself. On a hot, windy morning in June they donned "dry" suits of rubber-coated cloth over the conventional "wet" diving suits of foam rubber —and woolen underwear and socks as well—to protect themselves from the near-freezing waters to which they would descend. Then they climbed aboard a small diving platform which was to be lowered from a raft by a thin cable. Hannes Keller's friends held the cable, and Dr. Buhlmann was also aboard the raft, having come from Zurich to lend assistance.

In just three-and-a-half minutes, using three different mixtures of gases at various stages, they reached their goal in the depths, and after a brief pause they ascended to the surface in fifty-one minutes—the round trip taking only sixty minutes in all! And the depth gauge showed that they had gone even deeper than planned—to 723 feet—a new world's record.

This was 123 feet deeper than the previous record set by George Wookey in 1956, and their whole journey took only a fraction of the time required for Wookey to decompress.

Using his technique, of which the exact details still are secret, Hannes Keller feels that it will be practicable for divers without protective armor to work at depths of at least 1,000 feet and perhaps as far down as 3,000 feet. One of his main ambitions is to prove that his method will open up to exploration and development the continental shelf, the great undersea area abounding in hitherto untapped mineral and petroleum resources. He is, he says, now lost to mathematics: "Now I call myself a scientist in skin diving."

BIBLIOGRAPHY

EDMOND HALLEY

Aubrey, John. *'Brief Lives,' chiefly of Contemporaries, set down by John Aubrey between the Years 1669 & 1696.* Edited from the Author's Mss. by Andrew Clark. Volume I. Oxford: Clarendon Press, 1898.

Chapman, S. *Edmond Halley as Physical Geographer and the Story of His Charts.* London: Royal Astronomical Society, 1941.

Halley, Edmond. *Correspondence and Papers of Edmond Halley. Preceded by an Unpublished Memoir of His Life by One of His Contemporaries.* Arranged and Edited by Eugene Fairfield MacPike. New York: Oxford University Press, 1932.

MacPike, Eugene Fairfield. *Hevelius, Flamsteed and Halley: Three Contemporary Astronomers and Their Mutual Relations.* London: Taylor and Francis, Ltd., 1937.

Biographia Britannica. Volume 14. London, 1757.

Philosophical Transactions Giving Some Account of the Present Undertakings, Studies and Labours of the Ingenious in Many Considerable Parts of the World. Royal Society of London. Volume 29 (July, August, September, 1716); Volume 31 (May, June, July, August, 1721).

Sky and Telescope. March, 1942.

ROBERT FULTON

Colden, Cadwallader D. *The Life of Robert Fulton.* New York: Kirk & Mercein, 1817.

Dickinson, H. W. *Robert Fulton, Engineer and Artist: His Life and Works.* New York: John Lane Company, 1913.

Parsons, Wm. Barclay. *Robert Fulton and the Submarine.* New York: Columbia University Press, 1922.

Sutcliffe, Alice Crary. *Robert Fulton and the "Clermont."* New York: The Century Co., 1909.

Thurston, R. H. *Robert Fulton: His Life and Its Results.* New York: Dodd, Mead & Company, 1891.

The American Historical Review. April, 1934.

Harper's New Monthly Magazine. June, 1882.

Life. July 18, 1955.

WILHELM BAUER

Beach, Alfred E., Editor. *The Science Record for 1876.* New York: Munn & Company, 1876.

Delpeuch, Maurice. *La navigation sous-marine à travers les siècles.* Paris: Félix Juven, 1903.

Gluth, Oskar. *Wilhelm Bauer: der Erfinder des unabhängigen Unterseeboots.* Munich: Hans Sachs, 1911.

Scheffel, Fritz. *Der Brandtaucher: Wilhelm Bauer erfindet das U-Boot.* Leipzig: Hafe & Koehler, 1941.

Sigleur, Johannes. *Griff in die Unsterblichkeit.* Leipzig: R. Vorgtländers, 1938.

Thies, Hans Arthur. *Der eiserne Seehund: Wilhelm Bauer, der Erfinder des U-Boots.* Munich: Knorr & Hirth, 1943.

SIMON LAKE

Lake, Simon. *The Submarine in War and Peace: Its Development and Its Possibilities.* Philadelphia: J. B. Lippincott Company, 1918.

———, as told to Herbert Corey. *Submarine: The Autobiography of Simon Lake.* New York: D. Appleton-Century Company, Inc., 1938.

Wilkins, Sir Hubert, and others. *Under the North Pole.* New York & London: Brewer, Warren & Putnam, 1931.

The American Magazine. January, 1930; May, 1935.

The Cosmopolitan. August, 1904.

Harper's Weekly. January 1, 1898; April 1, July 15, 1899.

McClure's Magazine. January, 1899.

New York Herald. January 9, 1895.

The New York Times. June 8, 10, 15, 1904; November 23, December 31, 1931; December 21, 1932; September 13, 1933; December 8, 1934; August 6, September 27, 1935; September 26, 1936; June 24, 1945.

Scientific American. January 8, 1898; March, 1943.

Time. July 2, 1945.

United States Naval Institute Proceedings. March, June, 1957.

The World's Work. April, 1928.

Information about John P. Holland may be found in *The Birth and Development of the American Submarine* by Frank T. Cable (New York: Harper & Brothers, 1924). Underwater photographs by Louis Boutan appeared in *The Century Magazine* for May, 1898.

(CHARLES) WILLIAM BEEBE

Barton, Otis. *The World Beneath the Sea.* New York: Thomas Y. Crowell Company, 1953.

Beebe, William. *Adventuring with Beebe.* New York: Duell, Sloan and Pearce, 1955.

————. *The Arcturus Adventure.* New York & London: G. P. Putnam's Sons, 1926.

————. *Beneath Tropic Seas.* New York & London: G. P. Putnam's Sons, 1928.

————. *Book of Bays.* New York: Harcourt, Brace and Company, 1942.

————. *Edge of the Jungle.* New York: Henry Holt and Company, 1921.

————. *Exploring with Beebe.* New York & London: G. P. Putnam's Sons, 1932.

————. *Galápagos: World's End.* New York & London: G. P. Putnam's Sons, 1924.

————. *Half Mile Down.* New Edition. New York: Duell, Sloan and Pearce, 1951.

————. *High Jungle.* New York: Duell, Sloan and Pearce, 1949.

————. *Jungle Days.* New York & London: G. P. Putnam's Sons, 1925.

————. *Jungle Peace.* Foreword by Theodore Roosevelt. New York: The Modern Library, 1925. (Original edition published by Henry Holt and Company, 1918.)

————. *Nonsuch: Land of Water.* New York: Harcourt, Brace and Company, 1932.

————. *Pheasants: Their Lives and Homes.* Garden City, N.Y.: Doubleday, Page & Company, 1926.

————. *Pheasant Jungles.* New York & London: G. P. Putnam's Sons, 1927.

————. *Unseen Life of New York as a Naturalist Sees It.* New York: Duell, Sloan and Pearce, 1953.

————. *Zaca Venture.* New York: Harcourt, Brace and Company, 1938.

Gillis, Adolph, and Ketchum, Roland, Editors. *Our America.* Boston: Little, Brown and Company, 1936.

Tracy, Henry Chester. *American Naturalists.* New York: E. P. Dutton & Co., Inc., 1930.

The Atlantic Monthly. June, 1918; November, 1927; March, 1933.

Harpers Magazine. April, 1933; November, 1939.

The Literary Digest. April 21, 1934.

The National Geographic Magazine. January, 1932; June, 1958.

Newsweek. May 30, 1949; October 29, 1956.

The New York Times. July 5, 1925.

Science. November 21, 1919; February 1, 1929; December 18, 1931; October 14, 1932; October 27, 1933; November 30, 1934; September 26, 1941; April 24, 1942.

Scribner's Magazine. January, 1917.

Time. July 4, 1949.

AUGUSTE PICCARD AND JACQUES PICCARD

Houot, Georges S., and Willm, Pierre Henri. *2000 Fathoms Down.* New York: E. P. Dutton & Company, Inc., 1955.

Piccard, Auguste. *Earth, Sky and Sea*. New York: Oxford University Press, 1956.

Piccard, Jacques, and Dietz, Robert S. *Seven Miles Down: The Story of the Bathyscaph* Trieste. New York: G. P. Putnam's Sons, 1961.

The American Mercury. February, 1954.

Life. October 12, 1953.

The Literary Digest. June 13, 1931; January 28, 1933.

The National Geographic Magazine. March, 1933.

National Geographic. August, 1960.

Newsweek. April 12, 1954; February 27, 1961.

The New York Times Book Review. February 5, 1961.

Skin Diver Magazine. August, 1961.

Time. July 8, 1946; August 18, 1947; October 12, 1953.

Welcome Aboard Bathyscaph Trieste. San Diego: U.S. Navy Electronics Laboratory, n.d.

EDWARD ELLSBERG

Ellsberg, Edward. *Captain Paul*. New York: Dodd, Mead & Company, 1941.

———. *The Far Shore*. New York: Dodd, Mead & Company, 1960.

———. *Hell on Ice: The Saga of the "Jeannette."* New York: Dodd, Mead & Company, 1938.

———. *Men Under the Sea*. New York: Dodd, Mead & Company, 1939.

———. *Mid Watch*. New York: Dodd, Mead & Company, 1954.

———. *No Banners, No Bugles*. New York: Dodd, Mead & Company, 1949.

———. *Ocean Gold*. New York: Dodd, Mead & Company, 1935.

———. *On the Bottom*. New York: Dodd, Mead & Company, 1929.

———. *Passport for Jennifer*. New York: Dodd, Mead & Company, 1952.

———. *Pigboats*. New York: Dodd, Mead & Company, 1931.

———. *S-54*. New York: Dodd, Mead & Company, 1932.

———. *Spanish Ingots*. New York: Dodd, Mead & Company, 1936.

———. *Thirty Fathoms Deep*. New York: Dodd, Mead & Company, 1930.

———. *Treasure Below*. New York: Dodd, Mead & Company, 1940.

———. *Under the Red Sea Sun*. New York: Dodd, Mead & Company, 1946.

Collier's. June 16, 1928.

Newsweek. August 17, 1942.

Popular Mechanics. March, 1933.

The Reader's Digest. March, 1944.

The Saturday Review of Literature. May 18, 1929; March 5, 1938.

Time. August 17, 1942.

CHARLES BOWERS MOMSEN

Ellsberg, Edward. *Men Under the Sea*. New York: Dodd, Mead & Company, 1939.

Collier's. April 15, 1939.

The Dolphin. March 10, May 12, 1961.

Look. May 13, 1958.

The New York Times. February 6, March 7, May 11, May 14, August 31, 1929; May 26, August 3, September 16, 1939.

Newsweek. June 5, 1939.

Popular Mechanics. August, 1953.

The Saturday Evening Post. May 28, 1949.

Time. June 5, 1939.

(WILLIAM) MAURICE EWING

Columbia University Forum. Spring, 1961.

Harper's Magazine. September, 1958.

The New York Times. February 26, April 16, 1961.

Newsweek. October 30, 1944; May 27, 1946.

The National Geographic Magazine. September, 1948; November, 1949.

PSA Journal. November, 1951.

The Reader's Digest. September, 1954.

Saturday Review. May 7, 1960.

Science. May 21, 1926; May 19, 1939; July 18, 1947; February 26, June 3, 1960.

Scientific American. December, 1956.

Time. January 26, 1953; April 4, 1960.

JACQUES-YVES COUSTEAU

Cousteau, Jacques-Yves, and Dugan, James, Editors. *Captain Cousteau's Underwater Treasury.* New York: Harper & Brothers, 1959.

Cousteau, Jacques-Yves; Dumas, Frédéric; Tailliez, Philippe; and others. *The Complete Manual of Free Diving.* New York: G. P. Putnam's Sons, 1957.

Cousteau, Captain J. Y., with Dumas, Frédéric. *The Silent World.* New York: Harper & Brothers, 1953.

Dugan, James. *Undersea Explorer: The Story of Captain Cousteau.* New York: Harper & Brothers, 1957.

Tailliez, Captain Philippe. *To Hidden Depths.* New York: E. P. Dutton & Co., Inc., 1954.

Cosmopolitan. January, 1960.

Holiday. September, 1955.

Life. November 11, 1950; October 22, 1956.

The National Geographic Magazine. October, 1952; January, July, 1954; April, August, 1955; February, 1956; March, 1958.

National Geographic. April, 1960.

The New York Times. March 1, 1953.

Newsweek. February 13, 1956; March 14, 1960.

Skin Diver Magazine. April, 1961.

Time. March 28, 1960.

Vogue. November 15, 1956.

Welcome to the Calypso. Washington, D.C.: National Geographic Society, 1959.

EDWARD L. BEACH

Beach, Commander Edward L. *Run Silent, Run Deep.* New York: Henry Holt and Company, 1955.
————. *Submarine!* New York: Henry Holt and Company, 1952.
Blair, Clay, Jr. *The Atomic Submarine and Admiral Rickover.* New York: Henry Holt and Company, 1954.
Library Journal. February 1, 1955.
Life. June 13, 1960.
National Geographic. November, 1960.
The New York Times. August 20, 1958; May 11, 1960.
The Saturday Evening Post. October 22, 1960.
Time. January 26, 1953; April 4, 1955.

HANNES KELLER

Life. August 4, 1961.
The New York Times. December 9, 1960.
Newsweek. December 19, 1960.
Skin Diver Magazine. February, 1961.

SELECTED SUGGESTIONS
FOR FURTHER READING

GENERAL HISTORIES OF UNDERWATER
ADVENTURE AND SUBMARINE VEHICLES

Cross, Wilbur. *Challengers of the Deep.* New York: William Sloane Associates, 1959.

Davis, Robert H. *Deep Diving and Submarine Operations.* 5th Edition. London: The Saint Catherine Press Ltd., 1951.

Diolé, Philippe. *The Undersea Adventure.* New York: Julian Messner, Inc., 1953.

Doukan, Gilbert. *The World Beneath the Waves.* New York: John de Graff, Inc., 1957.

Dugan, James. *Man Under the Sea.* New York: Harper & Brothers, 1956.

Larsen, Egon. *Men Under the Sea.* London: Phoenix House Ltd., and New York: Roy Publishers, 1955.

de Latil, Pierre, and Rivoire, Jean. *Man and the Underwater World.* New York: G. P. Putnam's Sons, 1956.

Pringle, Patrick. *Modern Adventures Under the Sea.* New York: Franklin Watts, Inc., 1959.

Shelford, Captain W. O. *Subsunk: The Story of Submarine Escape.* Garden City, N.Y.: Doubleday & Co., Inc., 1960.

Whitehouse, Arch. *Subs and Submariners.* Garden City, N.Y.: Doubleday & Co., Inc., 1961.

FREE DIVING, PEARL DIVING AND
DIVING FOR TREASURE

Bartlett, Norman. *The Pearl Seekers*. London: Melrose, 1954.

Benham, Clarence. *Diver's Luck*. Sydney: Angus and Robertson, 1949.

Blair, Clay, Jr. *Diving for Pleasure and Treasure*. Cleveland and New York: The World Publishing Company, 1960.

Bridges, Lloyd, as told to Bill Barada. *Mask and Flippers: The Story of Skin Diving*. Philadelphia: Chilton Co., 1960.

Carrier, Rick and Barbara. *Dive*. New York: Wilfred Funk, 1955.

Ciampi, Elgin. *The Skin Diver*. New York: Ronald Press, 1960.

Crile, Jane and Barney. *Treasure-Diving Holidays*. New York: The Viking Press, 1954.

Clark, Eugenie. *Lady with a Spear*. New York: Harper & Brothers, 1953.

Clarke, Arthur C. *Boy Beneath the Sea*. Photographs by Mike Wilson. New York: Harper & Brothers, 1958.

———. *The First Five Fathoms*. Photographs by Mike Wilson. New York: Harper & Brothers, 1960.

———. *The Coast of Coral*. New York: Harper & Brothers, 1956.

———. *Indian Ocean Adventure*. Photographs by Mike Wilson. New York: Harper & Brothers, 1961.

———. *The Reefs of Taprobane: Underwater Adventures Around Ceylon*. New York: Harper & Brothers, 1957.

Hass, Hans. *Diving to Adventure*. Garden City, N.Y.: Doubleday & Co., Inc., 1952.

———. *Manta: Under the Red Sea with Spear and Camera*. New York: Rand, McNally, 1952.

———. *Men and Sharks*. Garden City, N.Y.: Doubleday & Co., Inc., 1954.

———. *We Come from the Sea*. Garden City, N.Y.: Doubleday & Co., Inc., 1959.

Gilpatric, Guy. *The Compleat Goggler*. New edition. New York: Dodd, Mead & Co., 1957.

Hampton, T. A. *Master Diver*. New York: John de Graff, Inc., 1956.

Jacobs, Jake, as told to Sylvia Jacobs. *Marineland Diver*. New York: Dodd, Mead & Company, 1960.

Link, Marian C. *Sea Diver: A Quest for History Under the Sea*. New York: Rinehart & Co., Inc., 1959.

Nesmith, Robert I. *Dig for Pirate Treasure*. New York: Devin-Adair Co., 1958.

Owen, David M. *A Manual for Free-Divers Using Compressed Air*. London and New York: Pergamon Press, 1955.

Potter, John S., Jr. *The Treasure Divers of Vigo Bay*. Garden City, N.Y.: Doubleday & Co., Inc., 1958.

Rieseberg, Lieut. Harry E. *I Dive for Treasure*. New York: Dodd, Mead & Company, 1942.

Sweeney, John. *Skin Diving and Exploring Underwater*. New York: McGraw-Hill Book Company, 1955.

Tassos, John. *The Underwater World*. Englewood Cliffs, N.J.: Prentice-Hall, Inc., 1957.

Travis, William. *Beyond the Reefs*. New York: E. P. Dutton & Co., Inc., 1959.

FROGMEN, THE ATOMIC SUBMARINE, AND UNDERWATER WARFARE

Anderson, Commander William R., with Blair, Clay, Jr. *Nautilus 90 North*. Cleveland: The World Publishing Company, 1959.

Borghese, J. Valerio. *Sea Devils*. New York: Henry Regnery Co., 1954.

Fraser, Ian. *Frogman V.C.* London: Angus & Robertson, 1957.

Pugh, Marshall. *Frogman: Commander Crabb's Story*. New York: Charles Scribner's Sons, 1956.

Waldron, T. J., and Gleeson, James. *Frogmen: The Story of Wartime Underwater Operators*. London: Evans, 1955.

Young, Edward. *Undersea Patrol*. New York: McGraw-Hill Book Company, 1952.

OCEANOGRAPHY

Bascom, Willard. *A Hole in the Bottom of the Sea: The Story of the Mohole Project.* Garden City, N.Y.: Doubleday & Co., Inc., 1961.

Carrington, Richard. *A Biography of the Sea.* New York: Basic Books, 1960.

Carson, Rachel L. *The Edge of the Sea.* Boston: Houghton Mifflin Company, 1955.

————. *The Sea Around Us.* Revised Edition. New York: Oxford University Press, Inc., 1961.

————. *Under the Sea Wind.* New Edition. New York: Oxford University Press, Inc., 1952.

Cowen, Robert C. *Frontiers of the Sea: The Story of Oceanographic Exploration.* Garden City, N.Y.: Doubleday & Co., Inc., 1960.

Daugherty, Charles Michael. *Searchers of the Sea: Pioneers in Oceanography.* New York: The Viking Press, 1961.

Douglas, John Scott. *The Story of the Oceans.* New York: Dodd, Mead & Co., 1952.

Gorsky, Bernard. *Vastness of the Sea.* Boston: Little, Brown and Company, 1957.

Hardy, Alister C. *The Open Sea.* Boston: Houghton Mifflin Company, 1956.

Herdman, Sir Wm. A. *Founders of Oceanography and Their Work.* London: E. Arnold & Co., 1923.

Murray, Sir John, and Hjort, J. *The Depths of the Oceans.* London: Macmillan and Co., Ltd., 1912.

Ritchie, George Stephen. *Challenger: The Life of a Survey Ship.* New York and London: Abelard-Schuman Ltd., 1958.

Sullivan, Walter. *Assault on the Unknown.* New York: McGraw-Hill Book Company, 1961.

Sverdrup, H. U.; Fleming, Richard; and Johnson, Martin W. *The Oceans.* New York: Prentice-Hall, Inc., 1942.

SALVAGE

Eadie, Tom. *I Like Diving*. Boston: Houghton Mifflin Company, 1929.

Grossett, Harry. *Down to the Ships in the Sea*. London: Hutchinson & Co., Ltd., 1953.

Keeble, Peter. *Ordeal by Water*. Garden City, N.Y.: Doubleday & Co., Inc., 1958.

Masters, David. *Epics of Salvage*. Boston: Little, Brown and Company, 1954.

————. *When Ships Go Down*. London: Eyre & Spottiswoode, Ltd., 1932.

————. *Wonders of Salvage*. London: Eyre & Spottiswoode, Ltd., 1944.

Young, Desmond. *All the Best Years*. New York: Harper & Brothers, 1961.

See also Benham, *Diver's Luck* and Rieseberg, *I Dive for Treasure* under *Free Diving*.

UNDERWATER PHOTOGRAPHY

Craig, John D. *Danger Is My Business*. New York: Simon and Schuster, 1938.

Cross, E. R. *Underwater Photography and Television*. New York: Exposition Press, 1955.

Du Pont, A. Felix. *Under Sea with Helmet and Camera*. New York: Dodd, Mead & Company, 1940.

Rebikoff, Dimitri, and Cherney, Paul. *Guide to Underwater Photography*. Philadelphia: Chilton Company, 1955.

Schenck, Hilbert, Jr., and Kendall, Henry W. *Underwater Photography*. 2nd Revised Edition. Cambridge, Maryland: Cornell Maritime Press, 1957.

Williamson, John Ernest. *Twenty Years Under the Sea*. New York & London: John Lane, 1935.

See also books by Jacques-Yves Cousteau and Hans Hass under *Free Diving*.

INDEX

ABOUT THE AUTHOR

During his childhood Frederick Wagner spent many summers in the small Maine seaport where his great-great-grandfather, Zechariah Cutter, had built ships for more than forty years. There, from the older townspeople, he heard many firsthand stories of the sea and seafaring men. His brother (who now lives on the Costa Brava in Spain, skin diving nearly all year round) first introduced him to the wonders of the underwater world, and a visit aboard Captain Cousteau's *Calypso* in the fall of 1959 spurred him on to learn more about famous underwater adventurers. This book is the result.

Born in Philadelphia, raised in Moorestown and Haddonfield, New Jersey, Mr. Wagner received his M.A. degree from Duke University and then taught English at the University of Oklahoma and at Duke. After a stint in the army during the Korean conflict, he came to New York City, where he now lives. For the past several years he has been handling sales promotion for a major book publisher.

With his wife, Barbara Brady, he is the co-author of *Famous American Actors and Actresses*, which George Freedley, President, Theatre Library Association, has called "invaluable for young theatre aspirants and for all younger people who would like to know something about our great American theatre past and the actors and actresses who created it."